MW01166551

Be still.

Know that God loves you.

Rest in His presence.

Lois R Hoogewee

Psalm 46:10-11

Be Still & Know

Breath praying through loss

Lois R. Hoogeveen

WESTBOW
PRESS
A DIVISION OF THOMAS NELSON

Copyright © 2013 Lois R. Hoogeveen.

Cover Design by Kimberly J. Lamb.
Photo by James L. Hoogeveen.

All rights reserved. No part of this book may be used or reproduced by any means,
graphic, electronic, or mechanical, including photocopying, recording, taping or by any
information storage retrieval system without the written permission of the publisher
except in the case of brief quotations embodied in critical articles and reviews.

All scripture from New International Version, Copyright ©
1978 by New York International Bible Society.

WestBow Press books may be ordered through booksellers or by contacting:
WestBow Press
A Division of Thomas Nelson
1663 Liberty Drive
Bloomington, IN 47403
www.westbowpress.com
1-(866) 928-1240

Because of the dynamic nature of the Internet, any web addresses or links contained in
this book may have changed since publication and may no longer be valid. The views
expressed in this work are solely those of the author and do not necessarily reflect the
views of the publisher, and the publisher hereby disclaims any responsibility for them.

ISBN: 978-1-4908-0144-5 (sc)
ISBN: 978-1-4908-0145-2 (hc)
ISBN: 978-1-4908-0143-8 (e)

Library of Congress Control Number: 2013912350

Printed in the United States of America.

WestBow Press rev. date: 07/31/2013

Dedication

This book is dedicated to James LeRoy Hoogeveen, my beloved husband, the father of my wonderful children, and the papa of my precious grandchildren. You were my dearest friend, my spiritual leader, and my ministry partner. You loved me, encouraged me, inspired me, and provided for me.

Your life exemplified unconditional love, immovable faith, and unquestionable integrity. You served as a pastor for thirty-five years, loving God above all and your neighbor as yourself, preaching and teaching biblical truths with boldness, and training leaders to be grounded in the Word and skilled in leadership. Your servant-hearted leadership and ministry impacted many lives and will forever be etched on my mind and in my heart.

God gave me the privilege of being your wife for forty-one and a half years. I will always miss your smile, your companionship, your wisdom, and your adventurous spirit.

> *The time has come for your departure.*
> *You have fought the good fight.*
> *You have finished the race.*
> *You have kept the faith.*
> *Now there is in store for you the crown of righteousness,*
> *which the Lord, the righteous Judge awarded you on*
> *March 2, 2012.*
>
> —2 Timothy 4:6b-8a (adapted)

Jim and Lois Hoogeveen
December, 2011

Contents

Preface

Our world turned upside down and inside out when my husband, James Hoogeveen, was diagnosed with epithelial mesothelioma cancer. The magnitude and impact of this diagnosis were overwhelming. My husband, a man who seldom went to the doctor, a man who played basketball several times a week, a man who exhibited boundless energy, went to the doctor with a persistent cough and left with a diagnosis of terminal, stage four, widespread, aggressive cancer. All I could do was utter breath prayers, focusing on a single word or phrase and a related Scripture.

> "Breath prayers" are prayers that can be said in a single breath. By remembering them throughout the day, you can pray them many times a day. They are also called "Prayers of the Heart."

> These are prayers that you can practice praying on all occasions, continually, and constantly, partially by praying breath prayers throughout your daily activities. The breath prayer is not to stir God to action through repetition, but to bring more fully to our own consciousness during our daily work the presence of our Lord and Savior, Jesus Christ.[1]

Many kinds of losses cause one to grieve. The breath prayers in this book are not just for those who have experienced loss through death. They are also for those suffering loss from a broken marriage, rebellious children,

---

[1] Mike Johnson, *Listening Prayer* (Sugar Land: Ascending Leaders, 2009), p. 25.

betrayal, financial downfall, unemployment, chronic illness, or any other kind of situation that turns one's world upside down and inside out. I share this glimpse into my spiritual journey with loss, praying that God will use my story to help you more fully experience His presence as you traverse the challenges you face in this imperfect world.

Breath prayers carried me through my husband's fast and furious thirteen-week battle with cancer. Breath praying upheld me as I faced the reality that life goes on after the death of a loved one. My hopes and dreams were shattered when my husband died and I became the surviving spouse. In the silence of my home, during challenging days and lonely nights, I repeatedly voiced single words and phrases. This is how God responded:

> *Be still, and know that I am God.*
> —Psalm 46:10a

Challenges triggered specific breath prayers. Memories led me to focus on different words. I share these stories and experiences as the backdrops of each breath prayer. Breath praying calms my turbulent spirit and opens my heart to feel God's presence. Breath prayers help me navigate the starkness of the present and the mystery of the future.

Be Still and Know contains fifty-two breath prayers, giving you the option to focus on one word each week for one year. Space is provided at the end of each chapter for you to write your own breath prayer, using the probing questions and breath prayer words. At the end of the book, there is space for you to develop a personal breath prayer word list as the Holy Spirit speaks to you.

I pray that *Be Still and Know* will help you discover the power of breath praying and lead you into a more intimate relationship with Jesus Christ.

Lois R. Hoogeveen

Acknowledgments

The cover photo of *Be Still and Know* was taken by my husband, James Hoogeveen (1950-2012). The morning of that sunrise is referenced in the fortieth breath prayer, "Look to the Lord." The cover was designed by our daughter, Kimberly J. Lamb. I am blessed by her ability to communicate through artistic design.

My mother, Anna Van Driessen (1918-2012), wrote letters, news articles, skits, song lyrics, and historical accounts of her local church. She finished writing a book documenting our family history a few weeks before her death. I am forever grateful that she instilled in me a deep appreciation for the power of the pen.

My three children and their spouses—Jeffrey and Rachelle Hoogeveen, Joni and Paul Krueger, and Kimberly and Jeremiah Lamb—are my cheerleaders, faithfully encouraging me with their love and prayers. Thank you for blessing your mother. Paul and Rachelle served as my initial editors. I am grateful for their writing expertise.

My family and friends read my weekly breath prayers, prayed for me without ceasing, and persuaded me to publish this book. I appreciate the significant role they played in motivating me to make these breath prayers available to a broader audience.

Thank you, Dr. Mike Johnson and the Ascending Leaders organization, for teaching me about breath prayers through the small-group study, *Listening Prayer*.

Above all, I am humbled that my Heavenly Father might use me, in my brokenness and sorrow, to minister to others.

> *Praise be to the God and Father of our Lord Jesus Christ,*
> *the Father of compassion and the God of all comfort,*
> *Who comforts us in all our troubles,*
> *so that we can comfort those in any trouble*
> *with the comfort we ourselves have received from God.*
> —2 Corinthians 1:3-4

1

Courage

The Cancer Center is the last place we want to be. We parked the car, walked through the doors, and registered with the smiling attendant. We sat down and waited in silence for my husband's name to be called. We wanted to get this appointment over with. And at the same time, we didn't.

We were both composed on the outside, but experiencing emotional turbulence within. We were scared. And yet, we held on to hope. I do not know exactly what my husband was thinking during that agonizing wait in the reception area, but a cacophony of thoughts crashed around in my head: *My husband has a positive attitude. Even doctors say that is a big factor in overcoming serious illness. We might have to change our plans for the next six to twelve months. We can do that and then resume our ministry after his treatment plan is complete. We just need to be strong and courageous as we experience this bump in the road. Many have gone through cancer treatment and then resumed normal living. Cancer is not always terminal. My husband is basically a healthy man. He is resilient. My husband is a man of deep faith. I am sure God still has a lot of ministry for him to do on this earth.*

We breathed in and breathed out. Courage. We needed courage to hear and accept the diagnosis and prognosis that the doctor was about to present.

> *Have I not commanded you? Be strong and courageous. Do not be terrified; do not be discouraged, for the Lord your God will be with you wherever you go.*
>
> —Joshua 1:9

Lord, give me courage. What situation in your life terrifies you, causing you to feel anxious, afraid, and helpless? Write a short prayer asking God for courage and assurance that He is with you.

2

Believe

Our world has turned upside down and inside out. We received both good news and bad news.

Good news. Bad news. They often come hand in hand. This is especially true when you are getting a doctor's report. The good news is that the cancer has not spread to my husband's brain. The bad news is that my husband has stage four epithelial mesothelioma. He has multiple tumors throughout his body. Jim was exposed to asbestos, the cause of mesothelioma, during his college and seminary days when he did a lot of remodeling, roofing, and construction work. This seems like unfair payment for working so hard to provide for our family while he completed his education.

Today our breath prayer is believe. We hold on to what we believe. We believe God is in control. We believe He has the ability to heal if He chooses. We believe our times are in God's hands.

> *But I trust in You, O Lord; I say, "You are my God. My times are in Your hands."*
>
> —Psalm 31:14-15a

I know whom I have believed, and am convinced that He is
able to guard what I have entrusted to Him for that day.
—2 Timothy 1:12b

Lord, help me believe. Has your world been turned upside down and inside out? Do you believe God is in control? Write a prayer telling God what you believe.

3

Lavished

Many people are lavishing their love upon our family through prayers, visits, and acts of kindness. As I faced the reality of my husband's terminal illness, I appreciated and treasured the love he had always lavished on me. Jim found great delight in the Bible's description of God's love and grace being lavished upon His children.

I will always cherish that sacred moment when God took Jim's hand from mine and brought him to heaven. He is now being fully lavished with God's love. Minutes after Jim went to heaven, I pictured him smiling at his friend, Jesus, as they greeted one another, face to face. Our Heavenly Father is delighting in Jim, lavishing him with love, and singing over him with rejoicing. "Blessed is the man who perseveres under trial, because when he has stood the test, he will receive the crown of life that God has promised to those who love him" (James 1:12).

God quieted the violent storm of cancer within Jim when He took him to heaven. I pray that God will quiet the storm of grief that rages within my soul. My breath prayer is that I will be comforted in the knowledge that my Heavenly Father delights in me, His daughter, as He lavishes me with love and grace.

How great is the love the Father has lavished on us, that we should be called children of God! And that is what we are.

—1 John 3:1a

Then will I purify the lips of the peoples, that all of them may call on the name of the Lord and serve Him shoulder to shoulder. The Lord your God is with you, He is mighty to save. He will take great delight in you, He will quiet you with His love, He will rejoice over you with singing.

—Zephaniah 3:9, 17

In Him we have redemption through His blood, the forgiveness of sins, in accordance with the riches of God's grace that He lavished on us with all wisdom and understanding.

—Ephesians 1:7-8

Lord, lavish your love upon me. Thank God for lavishing His love and grace upon you. How do you respond to God's declaration that He delights in you, His child, and sings over you with rejoicing?

4

Death and Victory

There's an app for that. We hear it over and over in our media-driven world. Television commercials promote medications to treat every kind of ailment. Magazines advertise products and services to fix any kind of problem. Computer companies offer various programs, or "applications," to cater to our whims. However, there is no app, no medication, no product, and no service that can cure the grief of losing a loved one.

Death hurts: It stings. It stabs. It pounds. Medical scientists have formulated many types of ointments, pills, infusions, and injections to help one cope with physical pain. But what about the pain of loss that is off the charts of a one-to-ten pain scale? Is there anything that can dull the ache, reduce the throbbing, or heal the wound?

My hope for pain control and healing comes from the promises I find in the Bible. God promises to never leave me nor forsake me (Deuteronomy 31:6), to hear my cries (Psalm 40:1), to guide me (Psalm 43:3), to be my strength (Psalm 46:1), and to give me eternal life through Jesus' blood and righteousness (John 3:15, 16). As long as life continues on earth, we will experience the sting of death. Not one of us is exempt from it. That is why it is urgent for us to not only hold on to the blessed assurance of complete healing and victory over death through our Lord Jesus Christ, but also to help others claim this victory while there is still time.

My breath prayer is to hold on to my Redeemer, the One who has conquered death. The loss of my loved one may hurt for the rest of my life, but I know that freedom from earthly sorrow is coming and that the victory celebration will last for eternity.

> Death has been swallowed up in victory. "Where, O death, is your victory? Where, O death, is your sting?" The sting of death is sin, and the power of sin is the law. But thanks be to God! He gives us the victory through our Lord Jesus Christ.
>
> —1 Corinthians 15:54b-57

Lord, swallow death in victory. Are you experiencing God's promises in your life right now? How does the hope of victory over the troubles of this world and death affect the way you approach life on earth?

5

Be Still

My world is spinning out of control. I had to choose a funeral home. I had to select a casket. I had to plan a funeral. I had to decide where to bury my husband. I had to write thank-you notes for all the memorial gifts I received. I had to pack up my house so I could move. I had to decide what to keep and what to give away. I had to select paint colors, floor coverings, and light fixtures for my new house. I had to buy a washer and a dryer. I had to do all these things in a four-week span of time.

Who would have thought that buying the washer and the dryer would be the final straw? It seems an insignificant task in light of everything else that was happening at the time. And yet, that was what pushed me over the edge of my endurance. How should I choose which brand to buy? Should I purchase a front-load or a top-load washer? Should I get a washer with or without an agitator? Would I prefer a dryer door that opened downward or sideways?

Family and friends packed, cleaned, and did everything they could to help me during this difficult time. But they could not stop the turmoil that raged within me. I felt like my world was spinning as rapidly as an automatic washer's final cycle. I thought the spinning would never stop.

Like a washer thrown off-balance by a heavy load, my head and heart were overwhelmed by all the changes that were happening in my life.

Turning abruptly away from the busyness all around me, I went into what had been *our* bedroom but was now only my bedroom and shut the door. I wept. I cried out to God. I wrapped myself in the covers and clung to my husband's pillow. My racing heart slowed down. And then I heard it. A majestic whisper: "Be still. Be still and know that I am God." I began to breathe the words myself. *Be still. Be still and know. Be still and know that I am God.*

> *"Be still and know that I am God; I will be exalted among the nations, I will be exalted in the earth." The Lord Almighty is with us; the God of Jacob is our fortress.*
> —Psalm 46:10-11

Lord, calm my racing heart. What is causing your life to spin out of control? Do you hear God saying, "Be still and know that I am God?" What will it take for you to be still and let God be God?

6

Rejoice

Today is the last day I will live in our home. Tomorrow I move to my new house. I am sure it will take time for me to call the new house my home.

Before I shut the door to the home that we shared for over sixteen years, I reflected on the many people who entered our front door for Bible study, family gatherings, church meetings, celebrations, or an evening of games and goodies. Seldom did anyone leave without a cup or two of coffee and a piece or two of dessert. Today was a day for remembering and rejoicing. The walls in our home heard many stories, many prayers, and a lot of music. It was a place to laugh and cry, to pray and sing, to learn and be taught, to love and be loved, to forgive and be forgiven.

The rooms in our house held many memories of Jim. We began most days sitting at the table drinking coffee, eating breakfast, reading the Bible, and praying together. Then Jim read the daily paper, staying current with local and world news. I often heard him chuckle as he read the comics. He ended most days sitting in his recliner with a can of Planters cocktail peanuts, a good book, and the TV remote, watching prerecorded games of basketball or football. I have precious memories of him engaging in intriguing discussions with myself and others. I hear him praying with and for me, our children, our grandchildren, our extended families, and the people of our church. I see him playing in the yard with the grandchildren. I smell the "papaghetti" that became his special recipe as well as the steak and burgers he loved to grill. I feel him taking care of me as he did the yard work, helped with the cleaning, kept our vehicles and bikes in good running condition, managed our finances, and resolved my computer issues. I sense his calmness, wisdom, and resilience as we worked together in ministry. I remember sitting in front of the computer with him planning many wonderful trips.

My breath prayer today is to rejoice as I remember. Memories are what I have left of our past. I have many good memories. God has blessed me indeed. I lived in the same house from the time I was born until the day I got married. Since that day over forty-one years ago, I have lived in thirteen different houses and six states. I have many memories of the people and experiences that filled these years. I remember all the people who prayed for us after we received Jim's cancer diagnosis; giving me a new understanding of what it means to belong to the Body of Christ. I remember the family and friends who worked countless hours over the past few weeks to help me move out of our home and into my new one. Today I remember and rejoice.

Give thanks to the Lord, call on His name; make known among the nations what He has done. Sing to Him, sing praise to Him; tell of all His wonderful acts. Glory in His holy name; let the hearts of those who seek the Lord rejoice. Look to the Lord and His strength; seek His face always. Remember the wonders He has done.
—1 Chronicles 16:8-12a

Rejoice in the Lord always; I will say it again; Rejoice! Let your gentleness be evident to all. The Lord is near. Do not be anxious about anything, but in everything, by prayer and petition, with thanksgiving, present your requests to God. And the peace of God, which transcends all understanding, will guard your hearts and your minds in Christ Jesus.

—Philippians 4:4-7

Lord, I rejoice. What memories do you have that give you reason to rejoice in the Lord? How has God blessed you? How does praying rejoice from the time you get up until the time you go to bed change your day?

7

Grace

He is risen! He is risen indeed! These words echoed in my heart this morning as I remembered Jim opening many Easter services with this joyous exaltation. Today is Resurrection Sunday. Jesus is alive, and because He lives, Jim is living in his eternal home!

Reflecting on Jesus' suffering took on a new depth of meaning this week. As I thought about how difficult it had been to watch my husband suffer intense, stabbing pain, I was awestruck by the truth that my Heavenly Father watched His Son suffer and die because He loves me. "How great is the love the Father has lavished on us, that we should be called children of God" (1 John 3:1).

Saturday was a day of silence in Passion Week. I experienced deafening silence yesterday. With a broken heart, I shut the blinds, curled up in a chair, and read all the sympathy cards I had received. Wrapped in Jim's prayer shawl, I read for several hours, soothing my broken heart with comfort, strength, and hope from the beautiful verses, Scriptures, personal notes, and assurances of ongoing prayer.

I pray for grace. I need to continually remind myself of God's sufficient grace. I moaned to God this week, asking how I would ever be able to live without my husband. Then I thought of the Israelites. They had nothing to eat or drink as they wandered through the wilderness. God heard their cry and gave them manna. He didn't give them a week's supply; He only gave them enough manna for that day (Exodus 16). I need to remember this whenever I begin to feel fearful and anxious about my future. Bible teacher Beth Moore, in a lecture on the book of Deuteronomy, compares grace to manna. God will give me a manna-portion of grace for today; tomorrow He will have a fresh supply.

> *But He said to me, "My grace is sufficient for you, for My power is made perfect in weakness."*
> —2 Corinthians 12:9a

Lord, give me grace. What manna-sized portion of grace has God provided for you today? Pray for God to provide His sufficient grace for a challenging situation in your life.

8

Lighten and Enlighten

I always knew my husband took good care of me, but I appreciate it even more now that I have to take care of myself. This truth hit home hard and fast as, for the first time, I was forced to take responsibility for many things, and to do so alone. One of those daunting realities was the fact that it was tax season when my husband departed from earth.

Memories surfaced of animated conversations I had heard over the years as people bemoaned this annual responsibility. However, I also have memories of three men in my life who never seemed stressed by the task. In fact, I think each one of them enjoyed the challenge. When I was a teenager, I sat at the kitchen table with my dad, writing down lists of figures he dictated to me as he sorted through the year's well-kept farm records. Later, on visits to my husband's parents, I saw one local farmer after another bring stacks of paper to my father-in-law, who would prepare their annual tax reports. And finally, I remember Jim sitting at the table with his laptop in front of him, papers all around, entering all the data on the forms that the Internal Revenue Service required. I had always inwardly marveled at how the people who do taxes know what to do. My role during tax season was to keep the kids entertained, to make Jim coffee, to bake him sweet treats, and to sign my name on the appropriate line.

Changing roles from just signing my name to gathering and presenting information was overwhelming for me. My appreciation for people who are trained and paid to do this job grew exponentially! Just the process of collecting all the data and trying to figure out what I needed to submit caused me immense trepidation.

Low on emotional, mental, and physical energy, my anxiety level continued to rise. *How do I figure out which facts and figures are important to the Internal Revenue Service?* I hit rock bottom that day. I went to bed and had a restless night. I arose early in the morning, beginning the day by meditating on Scripture and praying to my Heavenly Father. The Scripture in my devotional book that morning was this: "Your word is a lamp to my feet and a light for my path" (Psalm 119:105).

I did not know of any guidelines in God's Word that would help me specifically prepare to meet with the tax accountant, but my spirit became calmer as I prayed for God to lighten and enlighten what I was doing. I continue to breathe this prayer, lighten and enlighten, as I approach many other things that I must do for the first time.

My husband did take good care of me. He is not here to do so anymore. However, I don't have to take care of myself alone. My Heavenly Father is walking with me, lightening and enlightening my path.

> *The Lord is my light and my salvation—whom shall I fear? The Lord is the stronghold of my life—of whom shall I be afraid?*
> —Psalm 27:1

> *The Lord will be your everlasting light, and your days of sorrow will end.*
> —Isaiah 60:20b

Lord, lighten and enlighten. What situation would you like God to lighten or enlighten for you?

9

Presence

Preparation is half the battle. Creating a strategy helps to relieve anxiety. No amount of preplanning could have eased the harsh reality of living alone and grieving the loss of my husband, friend, and pastor. I am thankful for the stamina God gave me as I moved into a different house and took responsibility for all the transactions and transitions that must be dealt with when a spouse dies. In spite of these accomplishments, waves of weeping and sorrow still crest in me at unexpected times and places.

The ache of sorrow is very deep, but the presence of God is very real. I experience God's presence more vividly than ever before. Shortly before He ascended into heaven, Jesus promised that He would be with us always (Matthew 28:20). I am not surprised by God's presence. However, I am amazed at the impact of His presence as I walk through the valley of the shadow of death. Knowing that God is here helps me to get out of bed in the morning and get to sleep at night.

Death is not the only kind of sorrow one can experience in this life. Deep sorrow may come from loss of health, relationship difficulties, loss of employment, financial struggles, or separation from loved ones. Whatever the ache, whatever the sorrow, holding on to the presence of God is one sure way to accept and survive the situation. We must surrender to Him, the One who is in control of every detail of our lives.

Moses struggled with his God-given responsibility to lead the people of Israel out of Egypt, where they had been enslaved for many years. He did not think he was up to the task. He did not think the people would listen to him (Exodus 4). He must have felt overwhelmed by the unknown path ahead. I feel a bit like Moses. Just as he felt inadequate and resistant to God's plan for him to deliver the people from Egyptian slavery, I am struggling with the reality that I have outlived my husband and I now have many new responsibilities as the surviving spouse. I had thought my husband and I would grow old together. Now I find myself facing a different kind of future without my soul mate. My plans have changed. I am overwhelmed when I think of my new status—widow. *Why, God*, I ask, *have you left me to live alone?*

God's response to me is the same as His response was to Moses. In His still, small voice, He says, "I have not left you alone. My presence goes with you." He promises all believers that He will be there for us, always and forever.

Presence. Over and over I breathe the word presence. God is here. I am not alone.

> *The Lord replied, "My Presence will go with you, and I will give you rest."*
> —Exodus 33:14

> *Fear not, for I have redeemed you; I have called you by name; you are mine. When you pass through the waters, I will be with you; and when you pass through the rivers, they will not sweep over you. When you walk through the fire, you will not be burned; the flames will not set you ablaze. For I am the Lord, your God.*
> —Isaiah 43:2-3a

Lord, help me feel Your presence. When have you experienced the presence of the Lord? Are you carrying an ache so deep and personal that you feel you are carrying it all alone? Ask God to make you more aware of His presence.

10

Watch

I have three phobias. I do not like being lost, being out in the rain, or driving in the dark. All three of these phobias merged into one experience this week. One evening I met a friend at the local high school to attend a play. During the play my anxiety level began to rise as I heard the rain beating on the roof of the theatre. It was still raining when I exited the building after the play. I knew I would now have to overcome two of my irrational fears to get home: walking to my car in the rain and driving home in the dark. I had only a short distance to go, but it would be my first time driving home alone at night. The unexpected bombshell was when I walked to the place where I thought I had parked my car and it was not there.

My first thought was, *Who moved my car?* But no one could have moved my car. *It must be a bit further from the building than I remembered.* I frantically walked up and down the rows of cars, pushing the unlock button on my remote over and over and watching for my car lights to blink. I saw lots of cars light up as other people found their vehicles, but I didn't see my car. I zigzagged back and forth between the rows of cars, drenched in rain and tears, feeling like an old lady looking for her car in the grocery store parking lot. I finally decided I needed to go back inside to hide in a corner until everyone else drove away. The last car standing in the parking lot would be mine. I walked back toward the building, still frantically pushing my remote button. Suddenly, I saw the lights flashing on a silver car. It was mine!

As I sat in my car, trying to get my emotions under control, I surveyed the parking lot. I noticed three things: the parking lot had numerous sections, my car was not as far from the building as I had thought it was, and I had exited from a different door than the one I had entered several hours earlier. Even though I had tried to watch out for myself, I felt like I had failed. Yet God had heard my frantic prayers and watched out for me by helping me find my car. Even when I was lost, even when I was wandering around the parking lot in the dark and the rain—even then, the Lord was watching over my comings and goings.

I have a picture hanging in my house with phrases from Psalm 121 to remind me that the Lord is always watching over me. I love His promise. However, I believe I must also be actively watching out for Him, heightening my awareness of what He is doing, and giving Him the glory for taking care of me even when I am lost, wet, and driving in the dark. This requires intentionality, especially on days when I wake up under a cloud of sorrow and when a downpour of grief floods my spirit throughout the day.

My breath prayer this week is that I watch for how God is at work in my life. Thankful that God is watching over me, I am praying that I will be aware of Him in all my comings and goings, no matter what change, challenge, or decision is before me. I hear Him saying to me, "I'm watching you as a loving, protective parent would a child." I am trying to remember to respond, "I'm watching You, too."

> *I lift up my eyes to the hills—where does my help come from? My help comes from the Lord, the Maker of heaven and earth. The Lord will keep you from all harm—He will watch over your life; the Lord will watch over your coming and going both now and forevermore.*
> —Psalm 121:1-2, 7-8

But as for me, I watch in hope for the Lord, I wait for God my Savior; my God will hear me.

—Micah 7:7

Lord, watch over me. When are you most thankful for God's promise that He will always watch over you? What will help you become more intentional about watching out for God?

11

Come

I want to quit my job. There is no job description for a surviving spouse. The unwritten list of responsibilities feels endless, and the reality of why I am in this position is intense. The ongoing ramifications of this new role are draining my energy and my emotional reserve. Just when I think I can cross something off my to-do list, another form needs to be filled out, more information is required to complete a transaction, or a new matter needs attention. Checking my cell phone log, I was shocked to see that I had spent over thirty hours on the phone in less than a month. Most of those calls were to 800 numbers; having become the primary contact person and having moved to a new address, I'd had to update account information with many different service companies and agencies.

Maybe you too want to quit your job, whether it is the job you are paid for or the one that comes with the relationships in and circumstances of your life. I'm sorry to say that quitting is not an option for me or for you. Instead, we need to decide how we are going to navigate the responsibilities that come with our roles. I am thankful for the support my Heavenly Father provides twenty-four hours a day, seven days a week.

My breath prayer over the past few days has been listening to Jesus say, "Come." Whenever I feel overwhelmed, I remind myself that He wants me to rest in Him. I need to come. He will do the rest!

What does this really mean? Coming to Jesus and seeking His rest is an act of submission and surrender. It's admitting that I need help. Soul rest is putting my trust in Him and having faith in His divine care.

Sometimes God uses other people to respond to my cry for rest. Sometimes God uses you and me to respond to another person's cry for rest.

> *"Come to me, all you who are weary and burdened, and I will give you rest."*
> —Matthew 11:28

> *"Come, all you who are thirsty, come to the waters."*
> —Isaiah 55:1a

Lord, I come. Is God asking you to go to someone who needs rest? Is God asking you to come to Him so that He can give your soul rest? How does Jesus' invitation to come to Him for rest encourage you whenever you want to quit a job for which quitting is not an option?

12

Remember

Flower shopping should be fun. But I didn't enjoy it this year. I wanted my husband with me shopping for flowers as we did every spring, picking out annuals to add to our perennial beds. I did not want to buy flowers to put on his grave but that is what survivors do on Memorial Day. Jim always took care of our flowers. Now I have the new responsibility of taking care of *his* flowers.

Memorial Day is a special time to honor the men and women who died in service to our country. It is also a day for families to remember loved ones who have died. Although remembering might cause one's emotions to churn and surface, it also soothes the griever's heart to hear others share their own memories of our loved one.

Why do we wait until someone dies to remember him? The best gift we can give to our parents, children, and friends is the sharing of our memories that honor them for who they are and how important they are in our lives. The best gift we can give ourselves is to search for and celebrate the lessons we learned from the struggles we faced.

God remembers us and He wants us to remember Him. He promised to remember His covenant with us (Genesis 9:15); in doing so, He remembers our sins no more (Jeremiah 31:34). We must remember that He made us, He carries us, He sustains us, and He rescues us (Isaiah 46:4). We are to remember the wonders He has done (1 Chronicles 16:12). The people of Israel built stone monuments so that future generations could be reminded of what God had done (Joshua 4:4-9). Remembering is important; it is in telling the story that we are able to give God the glory!

My breath prayer this week is that I remember. I remember that I am blessed to have had a loving, faithful husband for over forty-one years. I remember his legacy, which impacts the lives of his children, his grandchildren, and many other people of different churches and communities. I remember my godly parents. I remember my children, grandchildren, family, and friends. Over these past few months, I have been reminded that I am blessed to know Christ and to belong to His family. I remember that God is the creator and sustainer of my life. He promises to be with me, to give me strength, and to uphold me.

When my heart aches from the physical absence of my husband, I remember that he is in heaven, face to face with the One he loved and served. I remember the last words Jim wrote in a letter to our dear friends, just a few weeks before his death: "I close this by writing that our lives are truly in God's hands. Always have been. Always will be." He would want me to remember that.

> *Look to the Lord and His strength; seek His face always.*
> *Remember the wonders He has done.*
> —1 Chronicles 16:11-12a

> *So do not fear, for I am with you; do not be dismayed, for*
> *I am your God. I will strengthen you and help you; I will*
> *uphold you with My righteous right hand.*
> —Isaiah 41:10

Lord, help me remember. What are some of your cherished memories of loved ones? What legacy are you leaving for others? What has the Lord done in your life that is important for you to remember?

13

Take Hold

I'll take care of that. I heard these words from family and friends over and over as they helped me during these past months. I also heard these words from health care providers, insurance agents, financial advisors, and legal professionals. Although I prefer doing things for myself and helping others, I am willing to admit that right now, I do need help. I am deeply grateful for the personal and professional resources that are available to me.

In 2011, homes, businesses, and farmland were damaged or destroyed by the Missouri River flood, a flood that was triggered by record snowfall in the Rocky Mountains as well as near-record rainfall in Montana. All six dams along the Missouri River were forced to release greater than usual amounts of water through their spillways. My husband and I biked from the campground where we were vacationing to Gavins Point Dam. Like many others, we stood in awe of the power of these rushing waters, feeling the spray of the water on our faces as gallons of water tumbled and crashed with a mighty force.

I had a similar day this week when my own "Misery River" swelled, the floodgates opened, and my tears were released in maximum volume. Like a core of engineers, I rehearsed many possible scenarios over and over while I sought protection and damage control. My confidantes listened to me and shared experiences from their personal storehouses of insight, wisdom, and knowledge. In the late hours of the night when normally I would be asleep, God directed me to ponder: *What is my ability? What is my responsibility?* These two questions brought clarity to what I could and could not do to calm my internal storm.

God whispered to me, "I'll take care of that and I'll take hold of you." This can only happen if I relinquish control of the situation and trust Him to take care of it in His way and in His time. Surrender and submit. This is not easy for a person who believes she should be able to take care of herself, that it is her responsibility to take care of herself. Surrendering control to God does not come with a guarantee that the outcome will line up totally with our hopes and dreams. That is why we cannot surrender without submitting. I am praying this week that I take hold of God's hand as I struggle with my abilities and my responsibilities.

When God took my husband's hand from mine, He did not let go of my hand. In fact, He tightened His grip on it.

> *For I am the Lord, your God, who takes hold of your right*
> *hand and says to you, Do not fear; I will help you.*
> —Isaiah 41:13

Lord, take hold of me. In your life, is there a situation that you have neither the ability nor the responsibility to change? Are you willing and ready to let go of the situation, take hold of God's hand, and let Him take care of the rest?

14

Renew

Remodeling is messy. Remodeling projects stir up dust and dirt in a home. The whole house is often in a state of disarray for a long time. Projects typically take longer than you think they will; unexpected glitches lead to tweaking or totally changing the original plan. Cleaning the house's duct system could be a necessary aspect of the final clean-up task.

I had the heating and duct system in my new house inspected to determine if it needed to be cleaned. The furnace was only moderately dirty. However, the duct work was a different story. The inside of the vents were layered with lint, dirt, and drywall dust. Although everything looked good on the outside, there was a lot of dirt in the system that was affecting the air quality of my house. The duct professionals were equipped and ready to clean my heating system. I just needed to tell them when I was ready and they would do the rest.

Learning that the air ducts in my house were coated with dirt caused me to think about what was clinging to the inside of my emotional and spiritual system. *What does God see when He examines my life? Are there unhealthy attitudes and feelings seeping into my head and heart? What needs to be cleaned out to allow His Spirit to flow more freely through every thought I think, every word I speak, every action I take?*

The loss of a loved one forces a major remodeling of life. It is messy. The dust of death settles into every part of one's being. Some days, a grieving person feels that life will never get back to normal. It is exhausting to grieve. Hopefully, a remodeling project has an end. However, there is no completion date for grieving. Unlike a remodeling project, grieving is not something a person chooses to do; it is unplanned. Two things keep a person going through post-grief reconstruction: the Contractor who commits to staying on the job around the clock and the promise of a future home beyond expectations.

My life is being remodeled. The words of one of my favorite hymns, "Breathe on Me Breath of God,"[2] express my heart's desire: "That I may love the way You love, and do what You would do." This has not changed.

My breath prayer is that God will renew my spirit. My spirit needs to be in good shape for me to love what God loves and do what God does. I know that the remodeling of my life is stirring up extra dust. I thank God for His forgiveness and grace, for His purifying process that restores my heart, through which every aspect of my life is filtered. God is able and available to do the work. I just need to be willing to let Him do it.

> *Create in me a pure heart, O God, and renew a steadfast spirit within me. Restore to me the joy of Your salvation, and grant me a willing spirit, to sustain me.*
> —Psalm 51:10, 12

> *Even youths grow tired and weary, and young men stumble and fall; but those who hope in the Lord will renew their strength.*
> —Isaiah 40:30-31

---

[2]   Edwin Hatch, "Breathe on Me, Breath of God" (1878, alt.).

Lord, renew my spirit. What does God see when He examines your heart? What needs to be purified in you so that God can renew your heart, letting the Sprit flow more freely through your life and restoring your joy?

15

Faith

Get in line and jump off the board. Those were my instructions when I took adult beginner swimming lessons. Just putting my head under water sent me into a panic. Now my swimming instructor was telling me to climb the ladder up to the high diving board and to jump into the deep end of the swimming pool. Always wanting to please my teachers, I ascended the ladder and slowly walked to the edge of the board. My legs shook and my heart pounded. A line of swimmers stood at the base of the ladder, waiting for me to jump. I wanted to go back down the ladder, but I was not given that option. I still cannot believe what I did: I jumped! I, the scaredy-cat, jumped off the board into the deep water with a capped, empty, milk jug in each hand. I am a diving survivor who can testify that plastic jugs full of air do, in fact, help a person pop back up out of the water.

Jumping off the diving board with a jug of air in each hand was definitely a leap of faith for me. Although I was not sure I would surface without a dramatic rescue, I chose to believe in my instructor's assurances that I would survive. My descent into the pool of widowhood has also been frightening. Many days, I panicked just to have my head underwater; I felt like I was drowning in the reality of this cold, deep pool. Numerous times, when I thought I had made it to the shallow end, another wave of sorrow swelled and threw me back into a seemingly bottomless pit. I have had to dive into the deep end numerous times as I learned how to be a solo homeowner, how to worship alone, and how to fellowship without my best friend and life partner. I know that God is by my side. But truly, it is much easier to walk in faith when you have someone doing it with you, someone to talk to, someone with whom you can process the potential peaks and pitfalls. Many times in our marriage, my husband and I moved by faith into the zone of the unknown. We did it in tandem. Now I have to do it alone.

In the late seventies, a few years after my once-in-a-lifetime leap into the swimming pool, I heard the song, "He Didn't Bring Us This Far to Leave Us"[3] and immediately resonated with these words: "He didn't teach us to swim to let us drown." This is another way of God saying: "Never will I leave you; never will I forsake you" (Hebrews 13:5b).

God has been teaching me how to swim through the channels of life for a long time; He is not going to let me drown. The learning curve I now face is beyond my comfort zone. I feel like my head has been underwater for a long time, coming up only for an occasional breath. I am surprised, however, that I have gradually become more comfortable in the middle of the pool and have even found myself floating once in a while.

On this Father's Day, I honor two of my incredible faith instructors: my father, and the father of my children. Both of these men did more than merely talk about faith; they lived by faith. No matter what was going on in their lives, both my dad and my husband demonstrated deep trust that God would protect and provide. By the way they lived, they taught

---

[3]   Phil Johnson, "He Didn't Bring Us This Far to Leave Us" (Dimension Music, 1978).

me that faith and hope go hand in hand. You cannot have one without the other. Reflecting on what I learned from these two important men, I know that although I have been forced to dive into the deep waters of broken dreams, God has put a jug in each of my hands—one filled with faith and the other with hope.

My breath prayer is to live each day with faith. I am pondering these questions: *What does it mean to have faith when the canvas of my future seems blank? What does it mean to have hope when I know the course of my life is forever changed?* As a scaredy-cat swimmer in the pool of grief, I can only say that this week I feel a little less like I am drowning and a little more like I am learning how to swim.

> *Now faith is being sure of what we hope for and certain of what we do not see.*
> —Hebrews 11:1

> *In the same way, faith by itself, if it is not accompanied by action, is dead.*
> —James 2:17

Lord, give me faith. Are you drowning in the circumstances of your life? What is in your pool that is making you afraid? Are you ready to dive in, trusting that your faith and hope will help you eventually get out of the pool of despair, disappointment, and loss?

16

Wisdom

I am a list-maker. Lists help me remember what I need to do, who I need to call, where I need to go. They free me from the pressure of trying to keep track in my mind of all the little things that could so easily be overlooked. Checking items off as they are completed and finally throwing away a finished list feels good. Previously only optional for me, lists have now become a necessity for managing my life, ever since grief diminished my ability to focus and remember.

Imagine all the lists I made when I was moving from one house to another and assuming sole responsibility for every aspect of my daily living. Whenever I thought of something I needed to do, I wrote it down. It didn't take long to accumulate so many little pieces of paper that they became unmanageable. So I started writing down my lists in a notebook and highlighting items as they were completed. Three months later, one notebook is full of lists, mostly highlighted, and I am starting on my second notebook. Hopefully it will take much longer to fill!

The challenge of having too many pieces of paper led to a wise decision. My list notebook has become a useful tool for documenting details of my conversations with utility, medical, insurance, and bill management agencies. It is an encouraging record of tasks I have finished and hopefully will never need to do again. This notebook reminds me of all the people who have helped me personally and professionally. Looking through the lists of calls I have made, appointments I have kept, and details I have addressed, affirms that I have indeed had a steep learning curve but I have also accomplished a lot as I navigated through many changes these past few months.

Every day I pray for wisdom, asking God to keep me steadfast, clear-minded, and calm as I make significant decisions and do many things for the first time. I need to keep growing in knowledge, wisdom, and understanding—in both the practical and spiritual areas of my life. Pastor Chuck Swindoll defines wisdom as "the God-given ability to see life with rare objectivity and to handle life with rare stability."[4] This definition accurately describes how my husband approached life, and it is how I long to be in my life. I want to be wise about how I go about the business of life. Even more, I want to be wise in the way I approach and respond to the people and circumstances in my life.

Grief does not lend itself to objectivity or stability. The loss of any person, position, or thing that we value is traumatic and affects every aspect of our lives. I know that I need spiritual wisdom as I adjust to the challenges of a life I have not chosen. Isaiah prophesied that the Spirit would rest on the promised Messiah. I ask the Spirit of the Lord to also rest upon me, His child, and to develop in me His wisdom, righteousness, and faithfulness.

---

[4]   Charles R. Swindoll, *Living on the Ragged Edge* (Word Books, Waco, 1985), p. 208.

Oh, the depth of the riches of the wisdom and knowledge of God!

—Romans 11:33a

The Spirit of the Lord will rest on Him—and the Spirit of wisdom and of understanding, the Spirit of counsel and of power, the Spirit of knowledge and of the fear of the Lord—and He will delight in the fear of the Lord. Righteousness will be His belt and faithfulness the sash around His waist.

—Isaiah 11:2-3a, 5

If any of you lacks wisdom, he should ask God, who gives generously to all without finding fault, and it will be given to him.

—James 1:5

Lord, give me wisdom. Write a breath prayer asking God to give you wisdom in handling your relationships and circumstances.

17

Beginnings and Endings

Life has many beginnings and endings; a multitude of firsts and lasts. I have had many firsts and lasts this year, many beginnings and endings. The first breath of my grandson began a precious life. The last breath of my husband ended a beloved life. I moved out of the last home my husband and I lived in as couple. I moved into the first house I have ever lived in as a single woman. Jim has now been in his eternal home for four months. I miss him so much, and yet I would never want him to leave the place of glory where he now resides. My heart rejoices for him even as I mourn my own loss.

God knows all the beginnings and endings that we will experience in our lives. I am thankful that I do not know the firsts and lasts that yet lie ahead of me. God, in His wisdom, shields us with time. He comforts us with His presence in all these firsts and lasts and in everything that happens in between. My in-between days now are long and lonely. As the lump of loneliness expands and contracts in me throughout the day, I experience God's presence. "The Lord is close to the brokenhearted" (Psalm 34:18a).

The plans and dreams that my husband and I saw in our future are now erased. It is difficult to think about the firsts that are still ahead for me because I am unable to imagine even a vague picture of what those new beginnings will look like, or how I will feel. I am certainly being reshaped. My future is nebulous.

So many firsts and lasts surface for one who is grieving, whether he is grieving the death of a loved one or the loss of something important in his life. I am anxious about some of the firsts that are yet to come. I am sad about some of the lasts. Memories of firsts and lasts also generate other emotions. When I look back over my life, there are many firsts and lasts that I celebrate. When I look ahead to the unwritten story of my future, I believe that God will give me firsts that will indeed bring me joy and blessing.

Even when we are discouraged, we can be intentional about choosing to put our trust in God, the One who promises to be with us through all our beginnings and endings. The promise of His presence gives me hope. Although there is pain in the firsts and the lasts, although my future is different than what I thought it would be, although I may often feel downcast, I will *yet* praise my Lord and Savior. I have a treasury full of cherished memories. I have children, grandchildren, family, and friends who shower me with immeasurable love and kindness. God has blessed me with the richness of His love and faithfulness.

I will continue to have firsts and lasts. Some will be happy. Others will be sad. The God of Genesis through Revelation will be with me. I need to remember that the next time I am anxious. My life, from beginning to end, is in His hands.

> *I am the first and I am the last; apart from Me there is no God.*
>
> —Isaiah 44:6b

Why are you downcast, O my soul? Why so disturbed with me? Put your hope in God, for I will yet praise Him, my Savior and my God.

—Psalm 42:5

I am the Alpha and the Omega, the First and the Last, the Beginning and the End.

—Revelation 22:13

Lord, be in the beginnings and in the endings. What are some happy beginnings and endings in your life? What are your painful firsts and lasts? How did you experience God's presence in these beginnings and endings?

18

Rooted

I should have stayed home. If I had known that a walk through the neighborhood on a beautiful November day would lead to a root canal seven months later, I would have stayed home. I did not know what I was in for when I went for that walk. Catching the toe of my shoe on a ridge in the sidewalk, I took a nosedive into the concrete. The rest is history. After a few weeks, my cut lip, bruised eye, and swollen nose had healed; on the outside, I was back to normal. Inside my mouth, however, the root of my front tooth was damaged. My tooth was forever changed—changed, but not destroyed.

On that same November day, my husband went to the doctor because he had a persistent cough. The rest is history. Both of our lives changed drastically. His life is changed for eternity. My life looks the same, on the outside. However, on the inside it is forever changed. My heart is broken, but it is not destroyed.

Antibiotics healed the infection that developed from the trauma to my tooth. The swelling and bruises on my face went away, but the pain and discomfort lingered. There were days when I had no pain, whereas on other days, there was a persistent throbbing. It was no longer obvious to a casual observer that my face had been injured, but the dull ache remained, imperceptible to others.

That is also how I experience grief. The initial trauma is gone, but the long-term impact of my loss still causes episodes of swelling and tenderness in my inner being. I have ingested verses from the Bible like antibiotics to combat feelings of sadness and disappointment.

I had three different experiences with roots this week. My first experience was a visit to an endodontist, a dentist who conducts root canals. He drilled the damaged tissue out of my root and filled it with a substance that would anchor the tooth. I am grateful for him, a skilled professional who saved my tooth, and for the modern technology that kept my pain at a level of minor discomfort. My second experience had to do with destroying roots, not saving them. I extracted prickly thistles one by one from my backyard, working diligently to remove the entire root of each plant. Hopefully, this will permanently eradicate the obnoxious weeds from my lawn. My third experience was a family gathering that reminded me of the rich heritage in which I am rooted.

My breath prayer is that God will keep me rooted in Him as I recover from the distress of death and rediscover the joy of living. Many people have been influential in helping me to become rooted and established in the Lord's unfailing love. My parents, teachers, friends, and beloved husband each played a significant role in my spiritual development. Deep spiritual roots provide us with strength to endure the storms that turn our worlds upside down. We will encounter trials of many kinds while we live on earth. "See to it that no one misses the grace of God and that no bitter root grows up" (Hebrews 12:16). The impact of painful circumstances will change us, but it cannot destroy us if we are rooted in the love of Jesus, knowing that Christ and the fullness of God dwells within us.

I pray that out of His glorious riches He may strengthen you with power through His Spirit in your inner being, so that Christ may dwell in your hearts through faith. And I pray that you, being rooted and established in love, may have power, together with all the saints, to grasp how wide and long and high and deep is the love of Christ, and to know this love that surpasses knowledge—that you may be filled the measure of all the fullness of God.

—Ephesians 3:16-19

Lord, keep me rooted. What roots do you need to extract from your life? What roots need to be nurtured to keep you anchored and to help you more fully experience the love of Christ?

19

Comfort

"Downsize" is the buzzword for my generation. I did some major downsizing when I moved from our large, multi-bedroom home to my own comfortable two-bedroom home. Saving a few things that might be valuable to my children and grandchildren, I purged my shelves of most of the other stuff I once valued and enjoyed. I have not missed any of the treasures I gave away or threw out.

A camping trip was the target of my downsizing this past week. Instead of packing the camper with food, clothes, and all the paraphernalia one usually takes for a week by the lake, I flew from South Dakota to Michigan with one carry-on bag to join friends for our thirty-fifth annual camping week. This was possible only because of the graciousness and generosity of my friends, who collectively ensured that I lacked nothing.

Traveling light was not difficult. Camping without my husband was. I had to face the reality that I have downsized. Camping was always something we did together. In yet another setting, I was forced to face the stark reality that I have gone from *we* to *I,* from *ours* to *mine,* from *us* to *me.* It feels wrong. "Me" is "we" upside down. It is something that has happened in my life, not by choice. I miss my soul-mate, a treasure that I did not give away or throw out, but rather, that death took from me.

Many things about the trip were the same, except for the absence of one of us. The days were shrouded with an ominous hush. Although I enjoyed conversation, laughter, and hours of relaxation with my friends, I also had repeated episodes of feeling downcast and experiencing the depth of sorrow that has invaded my life. The pulse of loneliness is rapid and irregular, even when I am with people who care deeply for me.

Comfort came through my friends' words of concern and prayers for peace. They are also mourning the absence of someone they loved. How do people comfort those who are mourning? By listening, sharing, laughing, and crying together. This week was a tapestry of discomfort and comfort woven together. One side of this week was very messy, but the other side was a beautiful display of the Body of Christ. *Spirit of God, give me comfort.*

> *Praise be to the God and Father of our Lord Jesus Christ, the Father of compassion and the God of all comfort, Who comforts us in all our troubles, so that we can comfort those in any trouble with the comfort we ourselves have received from God.*
> —2 Corinthians 1:3-4

> *But God, Who comforts the downcast, comforted us by the coming of Titus, and not only by his coming but also by the comfort you had given him. He told us about your longing for me, your deep sorrow, your ardent concern for me, so that my joy was greater than ever.*
> —2 Corinthians 7:6-7

> *As a mother comforts her child, so will I comfort you.*
> —Isaiah 66:13a

Lord, comfort me. How are you comforted? Whom might God want you to comfort?

20

Restore

I had a dream. I was a blue-eyed, curly-haired little girl walking through the pasture on the farm where I had lived as a child. The ground was dry and cracked. My short legs were trying to keep up with the farmer I was following. I was hot, tired, and falling behind. The distance between us was increasing. I was afraid that I would lose sight of him and be left alone in the field—not totally alone, though, because there were cattle in the field. This actually added to my anxiety; I was terrified of those big animals. Fear that I would never return to the safety of my family in the big white farmhouse engulfed me.

My pounding heart suddenly quieted as the scene of my dream changed. I was no longer following the farmer but, still a little girl, being carried by this strong, yet tender, man. The fields were no longer covered with brown, crusty stubble. They were gloriously arrayed with wildflowers of many different colors. In a third scene, I was walking hand in hand beside the farmer, quietly chatting as we enjoyed a stroll through the field.

The details of this vivid dream, a dream that I had over twenty years ago, have recently become very real to me again. No longer driven by the urgent demands that I have had to deal with these past few months, my days are now more quiet. I am tired. I rest. I read. I reflect. I remember. At times I feel like that blue-eyed, curly-haired little girl walking through the pasture just east of our farmhouse. My world feels parched and withered. I feel anxious about the known and unknown realities of living alone, and the monsters of grief and change that now share my space. I wonder if I will ever again find the safe place where I once lived.

However, my thoughts cannot stay in these places of sadness, fear, isolation, and uncertainty. The second scene of my dream gives me a different message. My Shepherd picks me up and carries me, and there is color in my world. The wind gently blows and the Shepherd whispers words of love and peace in my ear. We stop, sit in the soft field of wildflowers, and drink from the canteen of Living Water. My thirst is quenched. For the moment, I am refreshed. I pray that God will continue to restore me.

Right now I need the Shepherd to carry me close to His heart. I trust that the day will come when I am strong enough to again walk by His side hand in hand, close to Him and always safe.

> *He tends His flock like a shepherd: He gathers the lambs in His arms and carries them close to His heart.*
> —Isaiah 40:11

> *The Lord is my shepherd, I shall lack nothing. He makes me lie down in green pastures, He leads me beside quiet waters, He restores my soul. He guides me in paths of righteousness for His name's sake. Even though I walk through the valley of the shadow of death, I will fear no evil, for You are with me, Your rod and Your staff, they comfort me.*
> —Psalm 23:1-4

Lord, restore me. Extreme heat and lack of rain result in barren land. What heat and drought are you experiencing? Are you walking alone, trying to follow the Shepherd, or is the Shepherd carrying you? How does the Shepherd restore your soul?

21

Guide

I can't do this. That was how I'd felt a number of years ago when our camping group hiked to the top of Harney Peak in the Black Hills of South Dakota. It is the highest summit in the United States east of the Rocky Mountains, yet somehow, I was forcing my nonathletic self up to the top. As my husband and I ascended the trail, I looked ahead, hoping that the top of the next hill would be the peak. Time after time, a stretch of path leveled off or even went downhill only to turn into a steeper incline. I stopped frequently to catch my breath, mop the perspiration off my forehead, and drink more water. My husband waited patiently, encouraging me and cheering me onward. "You can do it," he told me as we inched our way upward. Many times, I wanted to quit, but I didn't. I kept going. Alone, I would have lost my way, but surrounded by people I trusted, I could follow them upward, one step at a time. I was so relieved when I finally looked up and saw the peak. Our friends had made it to the top ahead of me, and they cheered me onward. Imagine the ecstasy I felt when I joined the others for a group picture at the summit!

It was a good thing that I did not know what still lay ahead. We took a different trail back to the base, a trail that was more challenging than the one we had taken to the top. Sections of the path were narrow and rocky. We had to step carefully lest we lose our footing and slide down the rocks.

As I made the steep descent, my toes pushed against the front of my shoes, causing excruciating pain. Several times, I wondered why I had thought I could do this. Finally, I sat down on a log to rest. That was when I saw the breathtaking granite pillars of the Cathedral Spires standing in their glory against the brilliant blue sky. I beheld God's creation from a perspective I could not have experienced from any other spot. The path downward did get easier, and I felt an incredible sense of accomplishment when we finally arrived back at the base. *I did it!* I thought. I climbed Harney Peak.

Life holds many I-did-it moments for us to recall with joyful feelings of accomplishment. Many of them will begin as I-can't-do-it experiences. The greatest challenges often turn into the greatest memories. Also, the support of a particular person is often what turns I-can't-do-it grumblings into I-did-it accomplishments.

Our journey on earth could be compared to hiking a mountain trail. No two people take the exact same path. Some people will take longer than others to reach the summit. Far from being level and straight, our life's trails often include our life's trials. The pathway of life has twists and turns, ascents and descents, but there is beauty all around us as we travel. We need to intentionally look for these blessings.

The road of life I started on years ago with my husband is now marked "Closed." I have been rerouted to an alternate road. The last few months were rugged as I walked along the trail of firsts and lasts, of embracing the new and releasing the old. More than once, I thought to myself, *I can't do this.* Then I heard words that gave me the strength, hope, and courage to keep going. I have maneuvered twists and turns. It seems there is always another hill to climb, another curve to traverse. Downhill stretches are also challenging.

On days when I am not faced with a mountain of must-dos, I find myself descending along the path of emptiness, loneliness, uncertainty, and confusion. *Where is this path leading? What will be around the next turn?*

How long is the path; how far does it go? At times, I feel the road will never level off. Maybe it never will. Alone, I would lose my way; I would quit. However, I have a Great Sherpa guiding me. I am breath praying that I will trust my guide all day long, whether my path is ascending, descending, rocky, or on level ground. He has promised to lead me to the very top, to the place where His glory dwells. He surrounds me with people who encourage and support me as I continue on both easy and challenging roads.

I have been asking God to open my eyes to see the beauty and the blessings that surround my life on this new pathway. I do not want to miss the spires of His Sanctuary that are all around me in the beautiful world He created. My route to the crest might have changed, but my ultimate destination has not. Imagine the ecstasy that our loved ones who have arrived at the Heavenly Summit ahead of us have already experienced. Imagine our own ecstasy on the day when we reach the pinnacle of glory.

> *You guide me with Your counsel, and afterward You will take me into glory.*
> —Psalm 73:24

> *Whether you turn to the right or to the left, your ears will hear a voice behind you saying "This is the way; walk in it."*
> —Isaiah 30:21

> *The Lord is my shepherd, I shall lack nothing. He makes me lie down in green pastures, He leads me beside quiet waters, He restores my soul. He guides me in paths of righteousness for His name's sake.*
> —Psalm 23:1-3

Lord, be my guide. What I-did-it moments do you remember and celebrate? Which people helped you make possible what you had thought impossible? What blessings have you experienced on your journey because you asked the Lord to guide you?

22

Clothed

I used to wear only designer clothes. From the time I was born until after I was married, I wore designer clothes. The designer was my mother. Every garment I wore was a product of my mother's creativity and skill. She taught me and my four sisters how to sew. We learned to follow the guide sheet as we pinned pattern pieces to fabric, cut them out, and then sewed them together, one by one, until the garment was complete. The tools of this craft include pins, scissors, sewing machine, needle, thread, and a seam ripper. Mom said we could not sew without a seam ripper. Sometimes we needed it to take apart something that we had sewn incorrectly. Other times we used it to undo seams that required adjustments to make the garment fit better. The iron was another essential tool for sewing. We learned the importance of pressing each seam as we assembled the pieces, and of giving the entire garment a final pressing to complete the project.

No fabric was wasted. Unused fabric was cut and sewn together to make beautiful quilts. Even the fabric of clothes we no longer wore was used in quilts. Many years later, those quilts are good conversation starters since they hold memories of clothes we made and wore when we were kids.

God is the Master Designer of my life. He has taken the fabric of my personality, my natural talents, and my spiritual gifts, and stitched them together with the people and experiences in my life to make me who I am. Over the years, the unique style in which He crafted me became comfortable. But now I feel like the garment of my life has been attacked by the seam ripper. Some of the stitches that had held me together have been severed, and the fibers of my very being are stretched out and weakened. I am pressed down by the hot iron of loss and change. Some days I feel like I am being scorched. Yet I know that this painful process does have the potential to open seams and flatten wrinkles in my life.

I wonder how God is going to redesign the fabric of my life. *What will the new pattern look like? What will be the same and what will be different? What will the new garment that is being made be used for?* I believe that nothing will be wasted. I do not know what kind of quilt will be designed from the scraps of my life, but I trust that it will have a purpose and a message for my children and grandchildren.

Although I am uncertain what the new tailor-made design of my earthly life will look like, I pray with gratitude to be forever clothed in His love and grace. He has prepared a robe of righteousness for me that will never fade or tear, a robe I will wear throughout eternity.

> *I delight greatly in the Lord; my soul rejoices in my God. For He has clothed me with garments of salvation and arrayed me in a robe of righteousness.*
> —Isaiah 61:10

> *Therefore, as God's chosen people, holy and dearly loved, clothe yourselves with compassion, kindness, humility, gentleness and patience. Bear with each other and forgive whatever grievances you may have against one another.*

Forgive as the Lord forgave you. And over all these virtues put on love, which binds them all together in perfect unity.
—Colossians 3:12-14

Lord, clothe me. How is the pattern of your life changing? What purpose might God have for you with this new design? What does it feel and look like to be clothed in garments of righteousness?

23

Soar

I like to travel. I have had the privilege of traveling to destinations throughout the world, including forty-six of the fifty states of our country, as well as ten other countries. Preparation and anticipation were important aspects of any trip. My husband enjoyed planning our excursions. The first step was deciding what days we could be gone and where we would like to go. Next, he chose the best mode of transportation to reach our destination. If we were going by car, he studied maps to compare different routes, factoring in whether we wanted the fastest road or the most scenic one, and whether we should take a different route for the return trip. If we were flying, he diligently looked for the most convenient and least expensive connections from our home to our destination.

Packing has always been a challenge for me, even after decades of traveling for work and pleasure. *What will I need? What might I want to have? How much can I squeeze into my suitcase? What am I willing to leave behind?* This challenge is greatest when I am travelling by plane. *Can I fit everything into my carry-on or do I do I need to check a larger bag?*

When I fly I am always grateful once I have made it through the security checkpoints and have reclaimed everything that I had to part with to get to the other side of the scanning machines. I find my gate and wait for boarding to begin. When my row or zone is called, I board the plane, confident that the itinerary is correct, that the pilot knows how to fly the plane, and that the flight will get me to my chosen destination. Seldom do I see the pilot, yet I trust him. I do not understand the mechanics of flight, but I believe the plane will lift me off the ground, carry me hundreds of miles in the air, and then bring me back down in another city, state, or country. Sometimes weather or mechanical problems mess with my plans, resulting in missed flights, the hassle of booking another flight, getting to a different gate, and waiting. Revised itineraries take extra time and extreme patience.

My husband and I enjoyed dreaming about future trips, places we wanted to see and things we wanted to do before we got too old to travel. We were excited about the opportunities and adventures ahead . . . until cancer moved in like a mighty storm and messed up our plans. My husband was escorted into Heaven. I was left behind to continue traveling on earth without him. I lost my travelling companion. Although it feels like everything has changed, I know that is not true. Heaven is still my destination. The cross is still my boarding pass. God is still my Travel Agent. He planned the itinerary of my journey before I was even born. "All the days ordained for me were written in Your book before one of them came to be" (Psalm 139:16b). I know He has purchased a one-way ticket to heaven for me. "For God so loved the world that He gave His one and only Son, that whoever believes in Him shall not perish but have eternal life" (John 3:16).

Although I cannot see my Pilot, I have faith that He knows what He is doing. I am still adjusting to my revised itinerary, but I believe that my Travel Agent—who, by the way, is also the Pilot—has a plan to help me find joy on the journey once again. I believe He will show me new places as well as bring me back to familiar ones so I can see them from a new perspective. *Lord, if I am going to soar with You, I need to let go of my bags filled with disappointment, sorrow, and despair.* I am checking in my bags so I can be free to soar like an eagle with my everlasting God.

Do you not know? Have you not heard? The Lord is the everlasting God, the Creator of the ends of the earth. He will not grow tired or weary, and His understanding no one can fathom. He gives strength to the weary and increases the power of the weak. Even youths grow tired and weary, and young men stumble and fall; but those who hope in the Lord will renew their strength. They will soar on wings like eagles, they will run and not grow weary, they will walk and not be faint.

—Isaiah 40:28-31

Lord, help me soar. What could you empty out of your baggage to lighten your load? Where do you think the Lord will bring you when you choose to soar with Him?

24

How Long

How much longer will it take? Our kids asked these questions repeatedly as we travelled the interstates and highways en route to visiting their grandparents and cousins. Although I did not always voice it, I, too, felt like some of those trips would never end. This was especially true when we had to travel through blizzards, thunderstorms, blazing heat, or frigid cold. The conditions around me often influence the condition within me.

How long, O Lord? I ask this question over and over, sometimes aloud and sometimes silently as I limp through days of struggle, sickness, death, and grief. *How long, O Lord? How long must I wrestle with my thoughts and every day have sorrow in my heart?* (Psalm 13:2) My husband is gone from this life. He is in glory. I am left with a huge void in my life. *How long will this pain last?*

In some ways it seems that death visited long ago, so I should no longer be feeling so much sorrow. There have been times when the sadness was less intense. Then this week came along with a *wham* as different situations again ripped open my heart and soul. God does not answer my questions. He does not tell me whether it will be over in a week, a month, or a year. But what I do hear is God's majestic whisper: "I am with you." How do I know God has not forsaken me? I hear it in His Word. I feel it in my soul. I experience the presence of God through calls, visits, and emails from family and friends. Never underestimate how you, as a member of the Body of Christ, are the hands and feet of Jesus on earth. Although I do not understand the mystery of prayer, I believe in its power. Days I had anticipated would be unbearable have been just the opposite; I experienced inexplicable strength, comfort, and peace. I believe without a doubt this was because God was responding to the prayers of His people. I have received good returns on everyone's prayer investments.

How long, Lord? I ask. I believe my grieving will never be done. I think it is a condition that I will live with for the rest of my life. Dr. Jim Conway, a man of great faith whose heart was broken when his daughter lost her leg to cancer, compares losing a spouse to losing a limb. One might never fully recover, but you can adjust. That process takes hard work, determination, and time. No two cases are the same. There is no exact protocol that will work for everyone. Even after you've healed, you will not be the same. Loss leaves scars that last a lifetime. Grief changes people. I believe the symptoms of grief will eventually become less intense and the frequency of their appearance will decrease. I believe there will be days when I do not feel sorrow in my heart. I believe that the Lord God is always with me. I believe that He can take away my fear, my sorrow, and my emptiness, and in its place, fill me with His presence and His peace.

> *How long must I wrestle with my thoughts and every day have sorrow in my heart? Look on me and answer, O Lord my God. But I trust in Your unfailing love; my heart rejoices in Your salvation. I will sing to the Lord, for He has been good to me.*
> —Psalm 13:2a, 3a, 5-6

"Fear not, for I have redeemed you; I have called you by name; you are mine. When you pass through the waters, I will be with you; and when you pass through the rivers, they will not sweep over you. When you walk through the fire, you will not be burned; the flames will not set you ablaze. For I am the Lord, your God . . . Do not be afraid, for I am with you.

—Isaiah 43:1b-3a, 5a

Lord, how long? What causes you to ask God this question? Do you feel God's presence? Can you see the goodness of the Lord in spite of the badness of your situation?

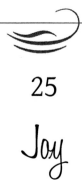

25

Joy

It is just an ordinary day. August 21st is just another ordinary day for most people. Not for me. On this day, I married a man whose life exemplified unconditional love, immovable faith, and unquestionable integrity. We each left our parents and promised to be faithful to one another "until death do us part". Death came sooner than either of us expected. Our sacred union of forty-one years, six months, and nine days was severed when my husband was taken from me to live eternally with his Heavenly Father.

Behind the sanctuary where we were married is the cemetery where my husband is now buried. The morning of our anniversary, I went to his gravesite. There, for the first time, I saw the tombstone that marks my husband's grave. It stands as a stately monument to the life and death of my beloved. In the quiet of the countryside, I sat in silence and solitude. I mourned. I wept. I lamented my loss. I rejoiced. I sang. I celebrated his gain.

We had always enjoyed planning and celebrating special occasions. How do I now commemorate the anniversary of my wedding day without my husband? I can't just ignore it, but how can I celebrate it? Right now, it is difficult for me to celebrate the present. I can, however, celebrate the past. I have albums and boxes full of pictures capturing snapshots of the wonderful life we shared for four decades. Memories and happy moments live in the heart forever. Becoming parents and grandparents, vacations with our children, family gatherings, camping with friends, overseas travels, ministering and teaching as a team, rejoicing and weeping with others, worshiping and learning together—these are just a few of our treasured memories. Our life together was richly blessed. Even in difficult times, the joy of the Lord provided strength.

Lamentation and celebration. Weeping and rejoicing. Weakness and strength. Odd combinations somehow create memorable moments. I am very sad, yet I have many reasons to rejoice. I had a husband who loved God above all and his wife, children, grandchildren, family, friends, and neighbors as himself. I learned so much from him about serving God with all my heart, soul, mind, and strength. He did not just teach these principles; he lived them. For so many years, he took care of me, provided for me, and challenged me to do things I might not have attempted without his encouragement. I continue to be blessed beyond measure by his influence. How do I honor my marriage? I pray for joy. I rejoice over what I had even as I weep over what I have lost.

The story of a widow named Naomi is found in the Old Testament book of Ruth. Naomi moved to Moab with her husband and two sons because their homeland, Bethlehem, was experiencing a severe famine. Naomi's life turned upside down when her husband and both sons died. Naomi was now a brokenhearted, grieving widow living in a foreign land. She decided to return to Bethlehem. As the people of her homeland welcomed her back, Naomi said, "I went away full, but the Lord has brought me back empty" (Ruth 1:21a). Indeed, the loss of her husband and sons left her heart more desolate than the barren fields and empty cupboards that drove her family out of Bethlehem a number of years earlier.

Like Naomi, I am both empty and full. My husband is gone but my mind and heart are filled with precious memories. I feel both weak and strong as I begin to embrace the changes in my life. While the absence of my beloved husband breaks my heart, I have a heightened awareness of the presence of the Lord.

My bridegroom has become the Lord's bride. I must rejoice with them! One day I will join their wedding party. That is a celebration I can anticipate with joy!

> *As a bridegroom rejoices over his bride, so will your God rejoice over you.*
> —Isaiah 62:5b

> *This day is sacred to our Lord. Do not grieve, for the joy of the Lord is your strength.*
> —Nehemiah 8:10b

Lord, give me joy. Are you experiencing a situation that makes you feel sad, frustrated, or helpless? Are you ready to ask God for His joy in the midst of your pain? How will claiming the Lord's joy and strength change you?

26

Know Jesus

What do you know? This might be asked casually, or it might be an expression of surprise. It might also be a challenging question in a serious conversation.

If someone had asked me this week, "What do you know?" my answers from one hour to the next would have been quite different. My thoughts and emotions soared to heights of peace and joy and also plunged to the depths of anguish and desolation over the week. I know that I need to accept the reality of my life. I did not have a husband to come home to after my four-day vigil over my dying mother. I did not have a husband to hold my hand as I said my final earthly good-byes to her. For the second time in six months, I placed the hand of a loved one in the hand of the Lord. I know that my husband and mother are both home with the Lord, rejoicing in His presence. I know that one day, I, too, will be safe in the arms of Jesus. Right now, however, I am grieving.

I know that God does not want me to dwell on my grief. I know I need to channel my thoughts and actions in ways that honor God and help me to move forward. But knowing is one thing; acting on what I know is harder. My breath prayer is that knowing Jesus will comfort and strengthen me as I journey from mourning to joy and as I await the day of my homecoming in heaven.

"What do you know?" is an important question. On his last New Year's Day on earth, one month after his diagnosis and two months before his death, my husband posted this on his CaringBridge website[5]:

A year ago I preached on one of my favorite passages, Colossians 2:2: "My purpose is that they may be encouraged in heart and united in love, so that they may have the full riches of complete understanding, in order that they may know the mystery of God, namely, Christ."

Throughout my life and ministry my purpose was, and continues to be, to enrich people's lives by helping them to know Jesus Christ and challenging them to grow in their relationships with Him. I know He loves me and will daily provide what is needed. That does not remove all the nasty things that go along with cancer, nor does it take away all the feelings of fear and sadness. But I do know that Jesus will be with us and help us every day.

I love the song "Knowing You, Jesus"[6] by Graham Kendrick. It focuses in a powerful way on the importance of knowing Jesus.

Knowing You, Jesus
Knowing You, there is no greater thing
You're my all, You're the best
You're my joy, my righteousness
And I love You, Lord.

---

[5]   Caring Bridge is a personalized website for those who are facing a serious illness. It provides a place for family and friends to stay updated and share words of love, hope, and compassion.

[6]   Graham Kendrick, "Knowing You, Jesus" (Make Way Music, 1993).

We ask you to join our breath prayer to know Jesus and to enrich the lives of others around you by helping them to know Jesus and grow in their relationships with Him.

—Pastor Jim

This is what the Lord says: "Let not the wise man boast of his wisdom or the strong man boast of his strength or the rich man boast of his riches, but let him who boasts boast about this: that he understands and knows Me, that I am the Lord, who exercises kindness, justice and righteousness on earth, for in these I delight," declares the Lord.

—Jeremiah 9:23-24

I know whom I have believed, and am convinced that He is able to guard what I have entrusted to Him for that day.

—2 Timothy 1:12b

Lord, knowing Jesus is a matter of life and death. The pastor who officiated at my mother's funeral service challenged family and friends with these words: "You are either in Christ or you are not. Are you in Christ? Do you know Jesus?" How would you answer these two questions the pastor asked? Is God calling you to help someone else know Him as Savior and Lord?

27

Persevere

It is the little stuff that often pushes me to the breaking point. Brewing morning coffee. Deciding what to eat. Sifting through the mail. Grocery shopping. Vacuuming. Washing dishes. Doing laundry. Watering the plants. Pulling weeds. Bringing the trash cans out and back in. Washing bugs off the car. Filling the car with gas. Closing pop-up ads on the computer. Changing the furnace filter. Not having anyone else to blame or complain to when I can't find something or when things get messy.

Partnered living has become solo living. Surprisingly, the weighty responsibilities like paying the bills, reconciling the checkbook, managing house, lawn, and car maintenance, and making financial and medical decisions are sometimes less stressful than the ongoing, never-ending little things. Not having help with the mundane tasks sometimes tips me into a melancholic state of gloom and doom. Even more disheartening is the absence of my sounding board and companion. The day-to-day chit-chat about what's happening in the church, community, or world, commenting on the beautiful sunrise, sunset, moon and stars, hearing Jim's thoughts on the weather conditions and their long-term impact—it is all missing. The absence of little conversations has been replaced by the echo of my own thoughts in an empty room.

Family dynamics have been changed by the loss of a father and grandfather. His absence is obvious, whether or not we talk about it with one another. Conversations, meals, and games are no longer the same. None of us can fill the gap of what this man contributed to our family. We have an empty chair. His absence is an ominous, deafening silence.

The death of a spouse, of a parent, of a child—each has a unique impact on the loved ones left behind. When a mother or father of young children dies, the surviving parent may become overwhelmed with being solely responsible for helping the children to process their loss, caring for their spiritual, emotional, and physical well-being, getting them to and from school and church activities, entertaining them, and teaching them life skills. The list goes on and on. How does a single parent find time to deal with all the little stuff in her kids' lives and still find time for her own personal grief? When children are left without a father or mother, who will fill that role in their life? How do children deal with the fears and anxieties that accompany the death of a parent? How will it impact them for the rest of their lives? And when parents grieve the death of a baby or young child, what do they do with the ache of seeing other children at the age their child should have been, learning to do the little things their child should have been learning? What do they do with the deafening silence of no more laughter or crying from their precious one?

We take much for granted. In marriage, couples develop an ebb and flow for life. We share and tweak responsibilities and develop routines that work for us. When death pays a visit, all those patterns are scrambled. It takes time to build awareness of the scope of being solely responsible for one's life. It takes time to accept the reality of being solely responsible for one's life. It takes time to learn all the skills needed to be solely responsible for one's life.

Some people have a natural bent for independent living. Others, like myself, prefer a team approach. Some people enjoy the unexpected, whereas others can be thrown completely off balance by it. Sometimes God allows us to be in situations that we would not have chosen ourselves. He uses those situations to help us mature and depend more fully on Him. It is on our knees, crying out to the Lord of Lords, that we grow in faith, self-control, perseverance, and godliness.

How do I deal with the little stuff? Some days, pretty well; other days, not so well. That's the precariousness of grief. It is unpredictable. It may be irrational. God does not wait for traumatic and dynamic situations to occur before showing up; He is there for the little stuff as well as the big stuff. He is there every hour of every day, every minute of every hour, every second of every minute. We seek God's help for the big stuff. Often, consciously or subconsciously, we try to handle the little stuff on our own strength. But truth be told, it's the little stuff that takes perseverance. The challenge to be godly is often greatest for the little stuff. Lord, help me persevere through the little stuff and the big stuff.

> *For this very reason, make every effort to add to your faith goodness; and to goodness, knowledge; and to knowledge self-control and to self-control, perseverance, and to perseverance, godliness; and to godliness, brotherly kindness; and to brotherly kindness, love.*
> —2 Peter 1:5-7

> *Let us run with perseverance the race marked out for us. Let us fix our eyes on Jesus.*
> —Hebrews 12:1b-2a

> *Consider it pure joy, my brothers, whenever you face trials of many kinds, because you know that the testing of your faith develops perseverance.*
> —James 1:2-3

Lord, help me persevere. How are you doing with the little stuff of life? With what do you need God's help to persevere? What is the blessing that comes with greater perseverance?

28

Purpose

Fixing puzzles is not my idea of a good time. I am not very adept at matching those tiny pieces and not very patient with the amount of time it takes to put together something that is just going to be torn apart afterward. Right now, I feel like a box full of disconnected puzzle pieces. What is God's new picture for my life—as it is currently being assembled piece by piece—going to look like?

"God can use you. He has purpose for your life." I find myself disliking the well-meaning words people say to me. I know they are saying exactly what I have said in the past to them or to other people. Interesting, is it not, how something can sound so profound when you say it to someone else, but so deafening when someone says it to you?

A year ago, this is how I would have articulated my purpose in life: *I am God's treasured possession who is passionate about my calling to encourage, support, equip, and release others to be who God created them to be and do what God created them to do.* For over twenty years, I have enjoyed leading women's Bible studies as well as training and coaching group leaders. My husband died in early spring. I had thought that by fall I would be ready to get involved again with various ministries and activities. It is fall now, but I am not jumping in.

My role in the church has changed. My focus in life has changed. My passion for serving has changed. I have encouraged many people to learn about themselves, to discover who God created them to be so they could do what God created them to do. Now I am resistant to the *who* and the *do* in my own life.

I do not hear God telling me what I am supposed to do. I realize that I do not want to find my purpose in life as a single woman. But like it or not, that is what I am. Deep down, I know that I do not want to just survive; I want to be revived. Rediscovering my purpose is difficult. It is painful. I am resisting because moving forward means letting go of a part of the past that I do not want to release: the pre-cancer past.

What is God's purpose for my life? Has it changed? Have I changed? He knew before I was born and He knew on the day I got married that the day would come when I would be alone with all the pieces of my life disassembled. Perspective is important when putting a puzzle together. Grieving can skew how one looks at things. A grieving person might dwell on the past and resist the future. We might focus on what we have lost without acknowledging what we have gained. We lose hope in the truth that, from God's perspective, what we are going through is exactly what He has ordained for us.

What have I gained? Above all, I have gained a deeper awareness of the presence of the Lord in my life from the moment I wake up in the morning until the moment I fall asleep at night. I have also gained a deeper dependence on God to get through the big and small stuff each day and week. I have gained freedom from fears that once weighed me down.

Each one of us is God's unique masterpiece and the pieces of our lives connect to create a one-of-a-kind picture. My prayer is that God will show me His purpose for my life that is now shattered by broken dreams. I know I need to depend on God to put my life back together, because I don't like fixing puzzles.

For we are God's workmanship, created in Christ Jesus to do good works, which God prepared in advance for us to do.

—Ephesians 2:10

Many are the plans in a man's heart, but it is the Lord's purpose that prevails.

—Proverbs 19:21

Lord, show me Your purpose. How are the pieces of your life fitting together? Do you know who God created you to be and what He created you to do? What is His purpose for you? How does that affect what you do and what you do not do?

29

Understand

Why? Why not? It's not fair. As a child you may have asked your parents these questions and pointed out to them how things were not fair. As a parent you most likely heard your children ask these same questions and bemoan the unfairness of life. It is sometimes difficult for children to understand their parents' choices, values, beliefs, and expectations. Fairness can be a big issue with children. Children who have learned to respect and trust their parents obey, even when they do not understand why.

Parent-child relationships give us a glimpse of our relationship with our Heavenly Father. We may find ourselves asking Him the same questions—"Why?" "Why not?"—or saying, "I don't understand." "This isn't fair."

My husband never asked why when he was diagnosed with cancer. Initially, neither did I. In the months following his death, though, I did ask why. *Why did God choose to take my husband to heaven when he could have ministered to people on earth for many more years, telling them about Jesus? Why did He not take me to heaven first? After all, my husband would have adjusted to life alone far better than I. Why did He allow so many people to be fatally exposed to asbestos?*

Your why-questions might be different from mine. "Why doesn't God answer my prayers for my child's health?" "Why did God allow my child to become a rebellious, prodigal son?" "Why doesn't God change my child's heart?" "Why doesn't God change my spouse?" "Why do I suffer so many health issues?" "Why doesn't God heal the broken relationship in my life?" "Why didn't God send more rain and less heat this summer?" "Why did God call us to move to a new place that is so far away from friends and family?" "Why do I struggle with finances when I work so hard and am a good steward of what I have?" "Why doesn't God help me get a better job?"

When our world turns upside down, it is no easier for us to understand the ways of God than it is for a child to persuade his parents to give him what he wants. One day, though, His ways might become more apparent. I can look back and see how God directed and protected me in different circumstances, like when we had to buy a different home while my husband was dying of cancer. I was disappointed that our offer was rejected for the first house we decided to buy. It did not seem fair that we were not even given an opportunity to make a counteroffer. My husband was getting radiation treatments every day. He had very little energy. We did not know how long he would live. I just wanted buying a house crossed off my list. But God was watching out for me. When we were too distracted to make a wise decision, He made it for us through a rejected offer. The house we purchased is newer, has a better floor plan, and is in a nicer neighborhood. I am thankful today for His intervention in this detail of my life.

God's ways are not always easy to understand. No matter what happens in my life, I choose to believe His promises. He promises to be my shield (Psalm 3:3), to guard me (1 Samuel 2:9), and to protect me (Psalm 91:14). He promises to give me wisdom (James 1:5), knowledge (Proverbs 1:7), and discernment (1 Kings 3:9). This insight will help me grow in awareness of His presence and will embed within me confidence, trust, and thankfulness that He is in control of every detail of my life. Lord, help me understand.

And if you call out for insight and cry aloud for understanding, and if you look for it as for silver and search for it as for hidden treasure, then you will understand the fear of the Lord and find the knowledge of God.
                                                                —Proverbs 2:3-5

Lord, help me understand. What are the why-questions you are asking God? What is your understanding of who God is and what He is doing in your life?

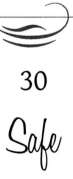

30

Safe

Be safe. I often said these words to my kids. Now they are saying the same words to their mother. "Lock the doors." "Leave the inside and outside lights on if you are coming home after dark." "Put a stick in the track of your sliding door so it cannot be forced open." "Always carry your cell phone with you, even if you are just going up or down the stairs, to the backyard, on a walk, or on a bike ride." "Lock the front storm door so you can see who is on your doorstep before fully opening the passageway into your house." Yes, I have heard a lot of advice about staying safe now that I am living alone—good advice. I appreciate their concern and experience and their suggestions to ensure the greatest measure of safety possible.

In the past I loved going out, meeting new people, spending time with family and friends, and seeing new places, both with my husband and alone. If I was alone, I knew that whether the experience was great or not so great, my husband would be available when I called him or when I returned home, ready to listen, celebrate, and support me. He was, indeed, my most valuable earthly security system.

I am surprised to find that now I do not enjoy going out and spending time with people as much as I once did. It often feels safer to be at home, secure within the walls of my house, rather than out in public. I struggle with the fear that I might not be able to control my emotions and that the people around me might not understand. When I do feel uncomfortable, whether I am at a worship service, social event, or family gathering, I no longer have the assurance that I can go home and fall into the arms of my safety net.

I had been thinking that this might be my personal grief issue. However, I have learned that it is not uncommon for people to feel less safe after the death of a loved one. I know there are many other situations that might also take away one's safe shelter. Loss, no matter what the cause, jolts one's security system and causes the person who is grieving to be more prone to worry and anxiety.

I believe it is part of God's divine plan for people to need people. After creating man, He said, "It is not good for the man to be alone. I will make a helper suitable for him" (Genesis 2:18). Being a person who processes information verbally, it is difficult for me not to have a trustworthy person with whom to share thoughts, experiences, blessings, and disappointments. Having lost the one person who served as my confidante, my sounding board, I need to reset my patterns of processing as well as to discover a different security system that works for my new status in life.

Praying the names of the Lord is one way for me to experience safety. The Lord hears me and cares about me. "He placed His right hand on me and said: "Do not be afraid. I am . . ."" (Revelation 1:17b). I feel His peace and presence when I remember that the "I am" is my Friend and my Counselor, my Protector and my Provider, my Watchman and my Shepherd, my Fortress and my Shield. He locks me in the safety of His love and lights the path that He has chosen for me.

> *The name of the Lord is a strong tower, the righteous run to it and are safe.*
>
> —Proverbs 18:10

Lord, be my safe place. To whom do you go when you want to celebrate good news, a victory, or something that fills you with joy? Where do you go when you need reassurance after stress or disappointment? Do you have a safety net? Are you a safety net for your spouse, child, sibling, or good friend? Which names of the Lord make you feel safe?

31

Stop, Look, Yield

Loss and recovery; fear and trust; sorrow and joy; tears and laughter; bitterness and forgiveness; despair and hope; isolation and interaction. These are some of the intersections on the road of life. Intersections are decision points. The choices that we make profoundly impact our lives. The choices we make determine where we end up and impact the experiences we have on the way there. We may decide to stop at one crossroad and consequently miss the opportunity that lies ahead at the next junction. For example, if we decide to stop at the "Mountain of Despair", we will lose the privilege of experiencing the rippling "River of God's Peace" just ahead.

When driving a vehicle, many intersections require us to stop, look, and yield. We may be in such a rush to get to where we are going, or so distracted by the intensity of life, that we forget to follow these road safety rules. Sometimes we get away with it, but other times, not paying attention results in consequences that we later regret.

Drastic life changes or overwhelming circumstances may cause us to move forward on autopilot. We go about the motions of life without thinking about what we are doing or why we are doing it. A goal might be as simple as getting something done so we do not have to think about it again. Caught up in the tyranny of urgency or the stress of reality, we might act or react without giving thought to what we are doing, or to what God is doing. The storm of tears and pain may become so violent that we are forced to stop moving. We cannot stop the storm, but we can protect ourselves from the dangers of the wind, hail, and lightening that attack our souls. We have the Word of God and the power of prayer to protect us, wherever we are and whatever the nature of the storm.

Stop. Look. Yield. *What is God doing in my life? Am I fully yielding to His control? Am I willing to submit my life to the Engineer of my life road?* I do not want to get stuck at the intersections of sorrow and tears, loss and doubt, fear and anger. I want to reach the junctions of security and safety, laughter and happiness, hope and joy. I have a great GPS to direct me as I traverse the highway of life on earth. My husband preached about God's Positioning Service, our spiritual GPS for our lives. It is important to pray that I remember to stop, look, and yield to God's Precise Strategy as well as God's Promised Support as I take a detour around the roadblock of grief and look for the new route God has already mapped out for me.

> *Stop and consider God's wonders.*
> —Job 37:14b

> *But if from there you seek the Lord your God, you will find Him if you look for Him with all your heart and with all your soul.*
> —Deuteronomy 4:29

> *[Yield] Submit yourselves then to God.*
> —James 4:7a

> *"Our Father in heaven, hallowed by Your name, Your kingdom come, Your will be done on earth as it is in heaven."*
> —Matthew 6:9-10

Lord, help me stop, look, and yield. What are the detours, roadblocks, and road closures of your life? What alternate routes have these obstacles forced you to take? Have you experienced any unexpected blessings by going a different way? Do you trust God's GPS for your life? Are you willing to stop, look, and yield to God?

32

Choose

We make many choices throughout the day. When we choose to do one thing, we are choosing not to do something else. Our actions reflect our choices. Our choices reflect our attitudes and our character. When circumstances are beyond our control, we choose to avoid, complain, react, or respond. When we are hurt by someone's words or actions, we choose whether to become bitter or better. Whether our choices are deliberate or subconscious, we live with their consequences.

Some things are beyond our control, like the ticking of the clock. Seconds roll into minutes, minutes into hours, hours into days, days into months, and months into years. When a loved one dies, we tend to want to live in the past. We would like to rewind the clock, but of course, that is not possible. We have to not only deal with the present, but also move forward into the future. This is life. We must choose what people, circumstances, and emotions we will allow to influence us during this difficult time.

I have been grieving for many months now. I am still learning so much about how loss impacts every moment of every day. Longing to hear, touch, and see the one who is no longer with me hurts. This is not just emotional pain; it hurts physically as well. Sometimes my body aches from the emptiness my heart feels. Tears blur my vision, often at unexpected times, and my eyes frequently hurt from crying, especially after a night of extreme loneliness.

Life is full of choices. The choices we make affect our present and our future. Loss hurts. I have choices to make about what to think and do if I want to heal from this pain and experience a brighter tomorrow. My loss is a part of my life. Likewise, your loss is a part of your life. I believe my loss will always be embedded in my heart and in my soul. However, I can choose whether or not to let my sorrow control every waking moment of my days. I must choose whether to nurture my sorrow and loss or to thank God for His presence, His grace, His comfort, and His mercy in the midst of my sorrow.

We can make choices that will help us finish well. A verse penned by writer Maria Robinson says, "Nobody can go back and start a new beginning, but anyone can start today and make a new ending." I believe this is how God wants us to live. Loss changes the ending. Right choices help us script an ending that will bring blessing and honor to the One who gave us the ability to choose. I am praying that I choose to live well so that I will finish well. I want to serve the Lord and walk in truth, even as I continue to walk through the valley of the shadow of death.

Choose for yourselves this day whom you will serve . . . But as for me and my household, we will serve the Lord.
—Joshua 24:15

I am Your servant; give me discernment that I may understand Your statutes.
—Psalm 119:125

May Your hand be ready to help me, for I have chosen Your precepts.
—Psalm 119:173

Lord, help me choose. What choices are you making to help you live well so that you will finish well? Ask God to help you make wise choices for both big and small decisions.

33

Fogged In

Fog? What fog? My sister was staying at my house while her husband was a patient at the hospital. She called to tell him she would be coming to the hospital a bit later than usual because she did not want to drive in the fog. "What fog?" he asked. Lying in the hospital bed only a few miles from my house, he looked out his window and saw a clear blue sky. But we could not see beyond my backyard. I called another sister, again commenting on the fog. "What fog?" she asked. There was no fog at her house either. Later, we ventured out, and just one mile away from my house, there was no fog. I realized then that my house is in a low spot where fog settles. I do not have to go far to get a clear view.

Grieving people live surrounded by fog much of the time. Everything closes in on you. You cannot see beyond your immediate surroundings. You think that others around you, or at least those closest to you, are experiencing the same thing. But when you venture out, you see people moving about freely. They do not have thick clouds hovering over them like the ones that linger over your dwelling.

Fog makes one's world very small. It does not feel safe to go out. When you do go out, you exercise extreme caution. It is hard to see others; you wonder if they see you. You feel vulnerable. The clouds that envelop your being make you dazed and disoriented. You hope you will not have to travel into unknown territory because you are not sure you will be able to see the road. It is nearly impossible to read road signs. Even familiar roads feel less safe than they once were. You wonder if others will be as careful as you are on the road. Driving in the fog and going out, enshrouded in grief, are very similar experiences.

I am living in a low spot physically and emotionally. I do not have to go far from home on a foggy day to enter a community that is enjoying clear skies. If I go out on a day when I cannot see beyond the sadness engulfing me, I am taken aback by the people who are laughing, interacting with one another, and enjoying life. There is no fog in their world.

An observation I have made about days that begin with a heavy fog cover is that they often turn out to be sunny, beautiful days with blue skies. I have experienced some of those days as well. I believe more will come. For now, I live in a low spot where the fog often settles. It is the season for fog. Some days, I will stay home until the fog lifts. Other days, I will leave home and hope to find a spot where the sky is blue, the sun is shining, and the heaviness has lifted.

I entrust myself to God since I am in this fogged-in state of grief. I imagine the clouds that engulf me as God Himself above me, before me, behind me, and beneath me, upholding me and guiding me through the day and through the night. Even in the fog, I will meditate on the presence of the Lord and rejoice in the assurance that He is with me.

> *By day the Lord went ahead of them in a pillar of cloud to guide them on their way.*
> —Exodus 13:21a

Praise the Lord, O my soul. O Lord my God, You are very great; You are clothed with splendor and majesty. He wraps himself in light as with a garment. He makes the clouds his chariot and rides on the wings of the wind. May my mediation be pleasing to Him, as I rejoice in the Lord.
—Psalm 104:1-2a, 3b, 34

Now we see but a poor reflection; then we shall see face to face. Now I know in part; then I shall know fully, even as I am fully known.
—1 Corinthians 13:12

Lord, I'm fogged in. What do you need to do when you are enveloped in the fog of life and cannot see beyond your own circumstances? How does God guide you?

34

Give Thanks

What do you say? Parents often tell their children to say thank you or to write a thank you note for a gift they received. It is important to parents that their children develop a grateful attitude and learn to express thanks for gifts and acts of kindness.

Even though we teach our children to say thank you, we adults sometimes have difficulty expressing thanks. What do we do when we receive something we do not need, want, or even like? Should we say thanks when we do not feel thankful? What if we forget to send a thank-you note, and by the time we remember it seems too late—then what do we do?

We teach our children to thank God in their prayers. Most adults find it easy to adore God for who He is. We thank God when He answers our prayers by giving us what we want. We thank Him for all the good things that happen. Can we be authentic with our praise when God does not give us what we want? Listing what I am thankful for this year feels paradoxical. *If I list the things for which I am thankful, does that nullify the reality of what I am not thankful for, namely, becoming a widow? If I praise God for His blessings and thank people for their acts of kindness, does that mean it is wrong for me to still feel sad and lonely? Is my gratefulness genuine if my heart still feels broken?*

God tells us to give thanks *in*, not *for*, all circumstances. Giving thanks is not just to be done once a year at Thanksgiving. Thanksliving describes a person who exemplifies an attitude of gratitude. It is a lifestyle choice. Being thankful may not come naturally to us, but it is a way of living we can choose to adopt. Giving thanks will not change our situation, but it will help us recognize the good that coexists with the bad. Looking for blessings, in fact, helps us build awareness of and appreciation for the gifts of mercy and acts of kindness that are indeed evidence of God at work through His people on earth.

There is much more to thanksliving than saying thank you when we get what we want. Thanksliving requires developing an attitude of gratitude. What is on my gratitude list this year? Since gratitude begins with attitude, I have to first of all ask myself, *What is my attitude this year?* Gratitude is a mindset, an outlook, a way of thinking. A grateful heart is like a lens through which one sees life; it affects the images we perceive. Gratitude begins by looking back. I am choosing to look back, beyond the disheartening realities of loss, to identify the reasons I have to praise God. I am thankful for a multitude of blessings that I have received through the pain and sorrow.

Giving thanks is not an option. It is a biblical command. Even in loss, even when your world turns upside down and inside out, there are many reasons to give thanks. When your heart is so broken that you cannot find the words to express thanks, there are resources to help you. The Psalms give us a language of praise. Many songs are wonderful expressions of thanksgiving.

Giving thanks is not conditional. The Bible does not say, "Give thanks when God answers your prayers by giving you exactly what you wanted." The Bible tells us to give thanks in everything. That means we must thank God on both good and bad days, in abundant years and lean years, when our children make us proud and when they disappoint us, in health and in sickness, in life and in death. Giving thanks does not change my situation. However, saying thank you helps me to feel more thankful, to recognize God's blessings, to appreciate others and, above all, to focus on the presence of the Lord. *Thank You, Lord. Thank You.*

> *Give thanks in all circumstances, for this is God's will for*
> *you in Christ Jesus.*
>
> —1 Thessalonians 5:18

Lord, I give thanks. Which of your attitudes needs adjusting so your life can become one of thanksliving? What is on your *gratitude* list?

35

Filled

I am so full. Have you ever said this after a big Thanksgiving dinner with your family? Did someone else say it? We stuff ourselves full of food at family gatherings and holiday parties and then moan as if we were force-fed. Why do we do it? We fill our stomachs to overflowing because we have an abundance of food right before our eyes, and because we enjoy feasting on such delicious fare.

It is not just our bodies that we overstuff. Many of us have filled our houses with so much stuff that there is no space left in our cupboards, closets, or drawers. It is not uncommon to moan and groan about all the stuff we have and our need to downsize. These conversations often take place as we shop with friends for another item of clothing or new piece of décor for the house. We fill our minds with both positive and negative thoughts, with useful and useless information, with important and unimportant data. We fill our days and weeks with things we like to do as well as things we would rather not have to do. We do things we do not feel like doing because it is expected of us, because it is our responsibility, or simply because these things need to be done.

People are overstuffed in many areas of their lives. When loss shakes one's world, turning everything upside down and inside out, most of this stuff does not matter anymore. Suddenly we hear the echo of hollow space and feel the void because the house is inhabited by one fewer person. The closets and drawers are emptied of a loved one's belongings. The calendar has one fewer person's activities filling the days. The tick of the clock is the only sound that fills the space as one hour slowly moves into the next.

We all make intentional choices about how to use our energy. Grief drains our emotional tanks at a rapid rate. A grieving person may stay home because her energy gauge is on empty. Like filling up at the gas pump, the cost of refilling our emotional tanks changes with time and circumstances. Refueling is a challenge. Sometimes we may need to have silence and solitude to fill our tanks. Other times we may need to be with family or friends to be re-energized. And then there will be times when we know our emotional energy is depleted but we are not able to identify the fueling option that would be best for us.

Very little has stayed the same in my life. How do I go about refilling the empty spaces? What do I want to replace? To add? To leave out? Asking myself questions is helpful during this season of discernment. *What are my criteria for making choices about what I will do and will not do? What will fill my emotional tanks? What will renew my spirit? Could this be something God wants me to do to restore joy and peace in my life and bring Him honor? How am I the same and how am I different from who I was before my loss? Am I willing to approach my new situation as an opportunity rather than an obstacle?*

I need to focus on filling my emotional and spiritual tanks. I am asking God to fill my spirit until I overflow with His joy, peace, hope, and power. I am praying to be filled with the fullness of God.

> *May the God of hope fill you with all joy and peace as you trust in Him, so that you may overflow with hope by the power of the Holy Spirit.*
> —Romans 15:13

And I pray that you, being rooted and established in love, may have power, together with all the saints, to grasp how wide and long and high and deep is the love of Christ, and to know this love that surpasses knowledge—that you may be filled to the measure of all the fullness of God.
　　　　　　　　　　　　　　　　—Ephesians 3:17b-19

Lord, fill me. What is turning your world upside down and stripping you of all the stuff you once thought important? What will you do to fill your soul with the hope and power of the Holy Spirit?

36

Beauty Out Of Ashes

Humpty Dumpty sat on a wall. Humpty Dumpty had a great fall. I have had a number of Humpty Dumpty episodes this week, times when my heart felt shattered into millions of pieces, and all my family and friends, all my prayers and Bible verses, all my grief support groups, all my books on grief and widowhood, all my sleep and exercise could not put it back together again. A broken egg is messy and difficult to clean up. It cannot be reassembled in the shell nor restored to its original shape and form. My heart is broken. It hurts. It feels messy. I wake up weeping, ravaged by memories exploding within me, unable to escape the debris of my life as the shattered pieces are splattered all around me.

I remember the day a shelf in my curio cabinet collapsed and several pieces of valuable glassware were broken. A skilled repairman was able to restore the candleholders my daughter bought for me in Egypt and the Depression glassware I inherited from my aunt. However, the china cup and saucer which were keepsakes from my grandmother's set of dishes, purchased in 1915, were shattered beyond restoration. They are forever gone from my life, except for my memory of them.

That's the status of my emotions this week: broken. Shattered beyond restoration. At least, that is how it feels right now. My only hope lies in the blessed assurance that there is One who restores broken hearts and is far more skilled than the artist who put back together the pieces of my treasured keepsakes.

Isaiah prophesied that the coming Messiah was One who makes beauty out of ashes as He cares for those who are brokenhearted and grieving. In all honesty, I must admit that I am apprehensive about the Lord making beauty out of the ashes of my loss. The very thought of beauty coming forth from the ashes of death stirs up the ache of walking away from the grave, exiting the cemetery gates, and leaving the remains of my beloved behind as I stepped forward into life alone. If the Lord turns the ashes of my loss into beauty, what will happen to the love I have for my husband? What will happen to my precious memories? How can something beautiful come from disease, suffering, death, and widowhood?

An egg often must be broken in order for it to be used. Breaking an egg reveals what is inside. I pray that what God reveals within me as my shell is broken will be put to good use. No one can fix a broken egg. No one can restore a broken heart to its original status. However, unlike an egg that is broken by an unexpected fall, the remnants of a broken heart do not need to be discarded. In fact, a broken heart can be used in new ways. My Humpty Dumpty episodes are part of my story, but not the end of the story. "The Lord is close to the brokenhearted and saves those who are crushed in sprit" (Psalm 34:18). I will hold on to the hope that He will take my ashes, my mourning, and my despair, and from them create beauty, gladness, and praise. I pray for Him to keep His promise to make beauty out of ashes.

> *He has sent me to bind up the brokenhearted . . . to comfort all who mourn . . . to bestow on them a crown of beauty instead of ashes, the oil of gladness instead of mourning, and a garment of praise instead of a spirit of despair. They will be called oaks of righteousness, a planting of the Lord for the display of His splendor.*
> —Isaiah 61:1b-3

Lord, make beauty out of my ashes. What example do you have of the Lord making beauty out of ashes in your life? How do you imagine He might restore your shattered dreams?

37

Expect

We all have expectations. We expect things of ourselves. We expect things of others. Expectations might be realistic or unrealistic, fair or unfair, just or unjust. We might say, *"I expect you to—"*, but more often, our expectations are unspoken. Identifying what our expectations are may reveal why we are struggling, disappointed, frustrated, or searching. Having realistic expectations of ourselves and of others is one of the secrets to experiencing contentment and peace.

How do we react to unexpected circumstances or unexpected responses from people? Do we feel angry, fearful, frustrated, devastated, or cheated? Seven months after my husband passed away, I got an unexpected medical bill. I was upset and frustrated. I expected the insurance company to cover this charge. They did not. While I was still brooding over this situation, I received another unexpected envelope. Inside was a check for a sum of money greater than the medical bill. That unexpected gift of love at just the right time was a resounding reminder of God's profound provision.

Expectations include an element of anticipation. What do you anticipate should or could happen as you make plans for Christmas celebrations? Plans often include family and friends, exchanging gifts, paying visits, and entertaining guests. Wrapped up within each one of us are many expectations. Some are obvious; others are hidden. Some will be met; others will not. Some people and gifts will exceed our expectations; others will disappoint us. Do you have realistic expectations as you anticipate your family's Christmas celebrations?

Waiting is another component of expectation. We wait for a baby to be born, for a house to be sold, for a job interview to turn into a job offer, for a doctor's report, for updates from family and friends, for an apology. It is in the waiting time that we develop character and that lessons are learned. Waiting often leads us to an increased awareness of God's presence and power.

I have been examining my expectations. *What do I expect of myself on this road of sorrow? What do I expect of others during my painful, confusing, twisted, and unwanted journey? What do others expect of me? What does God expect of me? What do I expect of God?*

God is the God of both the expected and the unexpected. Isaiah said of the Messiah, "You did awesome things that we did not expect" (Isaiah 64:3). Although the people of Israel were expecting His birth, they had to wait so long for the fulfillment of this prophecy that His incarnation caught them by surprise. Our own deaths and the deaths of our loved ones are expected events. Yet the timing and details are often unexpected. My prayer is that God will shape my expectations into realistic and joyful expectations of myself, of others, and above all, of Him as I live on earth and long for heaven.

> *Morning by morning, O Lord, You hear my voice; morning by morning I lay my requests before You and wait in expectation.*
>
> —Psalm 5:3

I know that through your prayers and the help given by the Spirit of Jesus Christ, what has happened to me will turn out for my deliverance. I eagerly expect and hope that I will in no way be ashamed, but will have sufficient courage so that now as always Christ will be exalted in my body, whether by life or by death. For to me, to live is Christ and to die is gain.

—Philippians 1:19-21

Lord, I expect. Are your expectations of yourself and others realistic? What are your expectations of God? Are you waiting for God to heal you? What are you learning as you wait?

38

Mystery

I enjoy a good mystery. Whether I am reading a mystery novel or watching a mystery movie, I like the suspense of the unknown and the development of a plot as it thickens and unfolds. I feel personal satisfaction when my prediction of the outcome or verdict is correct. I also enjoy the "I-didn't-see-that-coming" moment if the ending takes me by surprise. But as much as I like mystery in the world of fiction, I am not a fan of suspense in the real world. I do not like to be surprised by unforeseen circumstances.

Both birth and death contain many elements of mystery, drama, and suspense with numerous unexpected, untimely, unpredictable, and uncontrollable twists and turns. No two births or deaths are exactly the same. There is mystery in the survival of a newborn baby who enters the world too soon and too small. There is mystery in the loss of a loved one who leaves this earth suddenly and unexpectedly. There is mystery in a newborn taking his first breath. There is mystery in a loved one gasping for each breath and yet lingering day after day, week after week. There is mystery when a child's physical and mental development do not progress at the same rate. There is mystery in the loss of a loved one's memory and mental capacity while his or her physical body remains strong and healthy.

The story of each of our lives is being written by the Author of ...
Only He knows the details of our story from beginning to end. We know the day will come when life on earth will end. We might receive warning that our earthly life is almost over, or we might have an abrupt, unexpected ending. Unlike the length of a novel, the length of our story is unknown. We cannot know that the story will soon conclude because there are only a few more pages or a few more minutes left. However, those who believe in the Author and Redeemer of life do know *how* the story will ultimately end, even if we do not know *when* the end will come.

Sometimes life feels like a slow-moving movie. We do not have a fast-forward button for life. Neither do we have a rewind button. We do not have the option to skip pages to get to the end of the story. I wish there could have been more pages in the story of my husband's life, in the chapters of health as well as in the chapters of cancer. We never had a season of remission during which to rest and regroup and prepare for the imminent end. I wish we could go back a year or two to when we were both healthy and active and doing so much together. I wish we had talked more about certain things. I wish we had spent more time just being together. But going back is not a choice God gives us. Now I must learn to live each day anticipating God's plot for this new chapter in my life. Believing God has the mystery of my life under His control requires faith in the *I Am* of my life. "I am your Sustainer" (Isaiah 46:4), "I am your Provider" (Genesis 22:14), "I am your Protector" (Psalm 91:4), "I am your Friend" (John 15:15), "I am Sufficient" (2 Corinthians 12:9), "I am Lord" (Exodus 20:2)—these connect every word, every sentence, every paragraph, every page, every chapter of my story.

God wrote the beginning and the ending of each of our stories before we were even born. Our days are numbered. I am praying for peace in the unfolding of God's plans for my life, which are an unpredictable mystery to me. Even though I cannot fathom the mysteries of God, I know that "I am not my own, but belong—body and soul, in life and in death—to my faithful Savior Jesus Christ."[7]

> *He has also set eternity in the hearts of men; yet they cannot fathom what God has done from beginning to end.*
> —Ecclesiastes 3:11b

> *Can you fathom the mysteries of God?*
> —Job 11:7a

> *Oh, the depth of the riches of the wisdom and knowledge of God! How unsearchable His judgments, and His paths beyond tracing out! Who has known the mind of the Lord?*
> —Romans 11:33-34a

Lord, I am in awe of Your mystery. How do you feel about not knowing how the story of your life will unfold or end? How does knowing the Author of life give you comfort as you think about the mystery of your life?

---

[7] Zacharius Ursinus and Caspar Oleviannus, *Ecumenical Creeds and Reformed Confessions,* "The Heidelberg Catechism," p. 13, (Grand Rapids: Faith Alive Christian Resources, 1988).

39

Immanuel

What do you want for Christmas? This might be one of the most-asked questions during the last month of the year. Much of the Christmas season focuses on presents. Both young and old are wrapped up in the giving and receiving of presents. It is not uncommon to get a wish list from the people to whom we give presents. In fact, it has become quite normal and acceptable for wish lists to include websites and product numbers to ensure that gift-givers purchase exactly the right thing. Some people shop all year; they are already looking for presents for next year before this year's tree has even been taken down or the trash service has removed the packaging of this year's presents. Others wait until only a few hours of shopping time are left before purchasing items to wrap and put under the tree. Some people are careful to shop within their budgets. Others exceed their limits and suffer financial consequences for months.

I enjoy both giving and receiving presents. I love to find the perfect gift; I will shop relentlessly to purchase a present that fits the personality and interests of the recipient. I also enjoy getting presents, and feel an extra measure of pleasure when a gift reflects that the giver has considered who I am and what I enjoy.

My focus this year has shifted from *presents* to *presence*. The presence of my family and friends is the best present they can give me right now. Like a homemade gift that cannot be bought, presence is a gift that surpasses all others in value. In today's vernacular, we would say that it is priceless.

In the past I enjoyed decorating my house for the Christmas season. I had decided to boycott this tradition this year because I did not feel like celebrating, let alone decorating. Then something happened: I realized that I needed to celebrate the gift of presence, both in new ways and traditional ways. The small Christmas tree adorned with the baby shoes of each of our children and grandchildren is now set up, reminding me of the joy their presence brings to my life. Added to this tree is a new ornament, the word "Love", to remind me of a man who loved me, our children, and our grandchildren and who taught us all how to love God above all and our neighbors as ourselves. The wreath that my husband hung each year above our garage door is now in a new place with a new bow; it is the bow from his casket floral arrangement, and on its cascading ribbons are the words "Husband, Father, Papa." I look at it throughout the day and celebrate his presence in my life for so many years.

Above all, my appreciation for the presence of the Lord has risen to new heights. He is indeed my "Wonderful Counselor, Mighty God, Everlasting Father, and Prince of Peace" (Isaiah 9:6). Awareness of God's presence comforts me, strengthens me, gives me hope, and is my source of peace.

Immanuel—God with us: priceless. He is present in my life every day. God's budget for His presence is limitless. We may have as much as we want. It is a gift He is delighted to give. His presence is a perfect fit, a perfect match for whatever we need. His presence never needs to be returned. His presence is paid in full. It is a gift that we have in part now, but one day, the day we move to our eternal home, we will be in His wonderful presence in all its fullness and glory. Thank you, Immanuel, for Your presence.

"The virgin will be with child and will give birth to a son, and they will call Him Immanuel"—which means, "God with us."

—Matthew 1:23

Immanuel, God with me. What is a priceless experience you have had in the presence of family and friends? What is a priceless experience you have had with Immanuel, God with us?

40

Look to the Lord

Look at that! My husband and I often volleyed that exclamation between us as we ascended mountain roads, walked on sandy beaches, or spotted wildlife in open fields. We frequently summoned each other to the east-facing window or the west-facing deck at home so we could gaze together at a dazzling sunrise or a radiant sunset. "Look at that ominous sky." "Look at that full moon." "Look at all those stars." These shared moments are etched in my mind as cherished memories of standing together in awe of the Artist who created those scenes of indescribable natural beauty.

God gave us a memorable sunrise and sunset in the last year of my husband's life. The sunrise happened the morning we left the lake after our thirty-fourth annual camping week with dear friends. Shortly before we drove away from what, unbeknownst to us, would be our last time together at the lake, we stood hand in hand, mesmerized by a breathtaking, glorious sunrise. (This sunrise at Pleiness Lake, near Scottville, Michigan, was captured on film by my husband that morning and is the cover image of *Be Still and Know*.) Fast-forward five months: I had taken Jim to visit his parents, and father and son had said their earthly good-byes. The Lord graced our drive home with the most phenomenal sunset we had ever seen.

Brilliant sunrises and sunsets remind me of the Sovereign Lord who created life, who ordains the beginning and end of life and all that lies between the sunrises and sunsets of our days on earth. A brilliant sunrise erupts into the light of day. A breathtaking sunset is swallowed by the darkness of night. Life with someone we love is an experience that is bookended with sunrises and sunsets. At some point in life, we all release someone we love—a parent, a spouse, a child, a sibling, a friend—into the glory of the heavens. What we have left are some memories of majestic sunrises and breathtaking sunsets and a lot of ordinary days that now hold extraordinary value. Sunrises and sunsets now remind me of my husband and make me celebrate that he is in heaven, a place more glorious than the most magnificent sunrise or sunset, the most rugged snowcapped mountain, the most golden wheat field, the clearest lake, the fullest moon, or the brightest stars our eyes have ever beheld. When I look at a sunrise or sunset I hear God's voice saying, "Be still and know that I am God" (Psalm 46:10a).

Between the sunrises and sunsets of this past year, I have experienced the turbulence of storms. In many ways, it has been a year of exclaiming, "Look at that!" My rearview mirror reflects loss, grief, sadness, loneliness, change, and fear. However, that is only part of what is behind me. I also see love, grace, mercy, and peace. All these feelings and emotions are blended together, much like the colors in a spectacular sunrise or sunset.

It is important to pause and marvel at a year's worth of God-sightings. Making a list of all these aha moments and experiences is a valuable exercise. As I look back, I know without a doubt that it was the Creator of sunrises and sunsets, of mountains and valleys, of clear skies and stormy clouds, of lakes and dry land; the Author of life and death; the Giver of blessings in the midst of sorrow, who was taking care of me, His beloved daughter.

Life on earth, with all its joys and sorrows, is temporary. In my rearview mirror I see Jesus on the cross. I pause to say, "Look at that!" Jesus died in my place and now sits at the right hand of God. *Look to the Lord,* I breathe, and receive strength for today and hope for eternity.

> *Look to the Lord and His strength; seek His face always.*
> —Psalm 105:4

> *So we fix our eyes not on what is seen, but on what is unseen. For what is seen is temporary, but what is unseen is eternal.*
> —2 Corinthians 4:18

Lord, I am looking. What are your God-sightings that caused you to say, "Look at that"? How does seeing Jesus, first on the cross and then seated at the right hand of God, change your perspective on life?

41

Hold On

What will this day be like, I wonder? What will the future be? These words sung by Maria in *The Sound of Music*[8] express my thoughts as I begin a new year. At the end of a year we look back. At the beginning of a new year we look forward. Wondering what lies ahead might cause feelings of fear and anxiety. It might also trigger anticipation of new adventures and opportunities.

The year ahead for me will be a continuation of the extreme makeover that began for me last year. I know what the past looked like: there were positive, negative, and neutral experiences and situations. I have wonderful assurance of my future in heaven, and I look forward to it with eager anticipation. Right now I am thinking about the in-between time when I wake up each morning to live another day on earth. What will these days be like, I wonder?

I find myself in the center of tug-of-war living. There is a pull between fear and faith, doubt and trust, failing and winning, rejection and acceptance, being emptied and being filled, hanging on to the past and moving into the future, my plan and God's plan, death and

---

8   Rodgers & Hammerstein, "I Have Confidence" (R&H, 1959).

life, earth and heaven. Every hour of every day is filled with choices that will determine the outcome of this mental, emotional, and spiritual tug-of-war of life. Grief seems to amplify every aspect of this struggle.

What one holds on to determines the outcome of this tug-of-war. I need to repeatedly remind myself that I am not alone. I know that the Lord is there in the center with me. He has the power to pull me to the winning side. He has plans for my life on earth and He gives me hope for my life in heaven. I need to anchor myself to Him and hold on as He pulls me through day-to-day living on earth. Knowing that the Captain of the winning team is holding on to me helps me embrace the future with a measure of confidence and peace. "If God is for us, who (or what) can be against us?" (Romans 8:31b) I need to keep my eyes fixed on Him and remember to tightly hold onto Him so that I do not grow weary and lose heart as I begin this new year as a single woman.

What will this year be like, I wonder? What will my future be? I do not need to know all the details about what will happen in the year ahead because I believe in the One who promises to give me hope and a future. I hold on to the truth that I am His beloved, that He is sovereign, that my life is in His hands. Therefore, I live by faith, not by sight.

> *He reached down from on high and took hold of me; He drew me out of deep waters.*
> —Psalm 18:16

> *Love the Lord your God, listen to His voice, and hold fast to Him. For the Lord is your life.*
> —Deuteronomy 30: 20a

> *Yet I am always with You; You hold me by my right hand.*
> —Psalm 73:23

Lord, hold on to me. Although the details of your life are different from mine, perhaps you, too, would describe your life as an ongoing tug-of-war. What are you holding on to as you are pulled in opposing directions? On what do you fix your eyes as you react and respond to all that happens within and around you, when you are at the center of opposing forces? Are you letting God take hold of you?

42

Trust

I slowly ascended Mount Sinai, riding on the back of a camel. The Bedouin guide's English was probably limited to less than ten words. "Yes" had been the one he chose when I asked if Jamel was a gentle camel. Not only did I get separated from my husband, whose camel was farther back in the pack, but self-assured Jamel also got ahead of our guide. So it was just the two of us, Jamel and me climbing the narrow, rugged trail up Mount Sinai on a hot summer's day. Since Jamel was totally in control of this expedition in the Egyptian desert, I had to fully trust that I would be safe on his back as we slowly moved up the stony trail one step at a time. Jamel hugged the edge, and I wondered when his hoof would slip and we would crash down the rocky cliff. My heart pounded. I was scared. My racing thoughts slowed to Jamel's pace. *These camels must know what they are doing, or this Bedouin camel-riding business would have shut down long ago.* I cautiously put more trust in Jamel's instincts, relaxed a bit, and began to enjoy the experience. Jamel took me as far as he could go. Camels know their limits. No way was Jamel or any of the camels going to attempt the 750 steps hewn out of the mountain rock to get to the summit of Mount Sinai.

But bidding farewell to Jamel was not the end of my trust walk that day. After sunset, we had to go down the same rocky, windy, trail on foot and in the dark to return to our base camp. Our group guide lost sight of the path, so we had a taste of wandering in the desert in the black of night. My fearless husband persistently checked every potential path, and once he found the right one, he became our trusted Sherpa, leading our group safely back to camp.

I trusted the person who was initially leading our group until we all realized we were off the designated trail. Some people, like me, will trust almost everyone until anything happens to indicate a person is untrustworthy. Others will only begin to trust people once they have proven that they can be trusted. Which style of trust do you identify with? Without trust, relationships are compromised; we do not reap its full value. What are you doing to prove that you can be trusted? What are you doing to cultivate trusting relationships with others? Fear takes over in the absence of trust. When we find ourselves living in fear, we need to explore who can help us and what we can do to dissolve that fear. Only as we put our trust in reliable, honorable sources will we be able to calm our souls and develop a spirit of peace. Indeed, trust is the only antidote to fear.

Trust transcends human relationships. People will disappoint us. They will break our trust. Circumstances will challenge us and may become a source of anxiety and fear. But God will never abandon us, betray us, mislead us, or reject us. He is with us in every situation we encounter, in every trial we face. He wants us to strengthen our faith as we navigate our weakest moments and most painful experiences. Even when death takes those we love and with whom we had planned to spend many more years with on earth, even when we are disappointed that God's plan did not match our plan, even when we are fearful about surviving without our spouses, even when our world turns upside down and inside out—even then, we can still trust God. Our Heavenly Father does not promise to always give us what we want, but He does promise to never leave us or forsake us. He promises to be our refuge and our strength. Lord, strengthen my trust in You.

Trust, faith, hope: these three are intertwined. Trust is the backbone of faith, and faith is the foundation of hope. As we trust the Lord in the darkest night, our faith becomes stronger, and hope is birthed. Trust, faith, and hope are the benefits we receive upon believing in Jesus Christ. They are His gifts to us, His chosen, treasured people. No one other than our Redeeming Savior and Lord can give these to us, and no one can take them away. Trust, faith, and hope fuel us in the best and worst circumstances, in our strongest and weakest moments. In them, the Giver of these gifts displays His presence and power. The Lord is sure-footed as He carries me on the rugged path of life. I trusted Jamel, so doesn't it make all the more sense to trust Jehovah?

> *Trust in the Lord with all your heart and lean not on our own understanding; in all your ways acknowledge Him, and He will make your paths straight.*
> —Proverbs 3:5-6

> *When I am afraid, I will trust in You.*
> —Psalm 56:3

> *May the God of hope fill you with all joy and peace as you trust in Him, so that you may overflow with hope by the power of the Holy Spirit.*
> —Romans 15:13

Lord, help me trust. How would you describe your trust in others, and in God? How are trust, faith, and hope intertwined in your life? Where or when do you need to trust God more completely?

43

Radiant

Good morning, my daughter. I am here to be your light, warm your heart, guide your steps, and take care of you all day long. God was speaking to me. Not through a beautiful sunrise painted across the heavens like the one I had experienced a few weeks ago—this was different. This was a clear sky with the magnificent orange ball of the morning sun emerging in the eastern sky. Although I wanted to fix my eyes on that beautiful star, the largest in the solar system, I had to look away because the brightness was so intense. The sun is powerful. It gives me energy. On a day when the sun is hidden by the clouds, I feel more tired and less motivated. Even if it is cold, even if the ground is covered with snow, even if it is windy—if the sun is shining, I deal better with all those elements. What would I do without the sun?

Looking at the sun makes me think about how I am affected by looking at the Son of God. Am I as drawn to gaze at the Son of God as I am to gaze at the brilliant morning sun? Does His presence captivate me and cause me to stand in awe and to behold Him in all His majesty? Do I freely talk with others about the magnificent Son-rises I experience in day-to-day living? Just as we take the sun for granted, I fear that we also become apathetic to the Son in our lives. I know that I deal with life much better not only when I am blessed with a sunny day, but also when I am blessed with a keen awareness of the Son permeating every moment of my day.

People know when I have spent time in the sun. They can see it in my face; the color of my skin changes. Sometimes they comment on it and I am a bit surprised that it is obvious to others that I have been soaking up the rays. The Bible tells us of at least two instances when being in the presence of the Lord affected a person's countenance. When Moses came down from the mountain after receiving the Ten Commandments from the Lord, the people could see that he had absorbed a lot of Son-rays. He didn't even realize it himself. Moses had been with the Lord and his face was radiant (Exodus 34:29). The Bible tells us that at the Transfiguration, Jesus' face shone like the sun (Matthew 17:2). Interesting: the *Son's* face shone like the *sun*.

We might pray for the sun to shine again after several cloudy, dreary days. Do we ask God to shine His face upon us and give us peace, to brighten up our world, when we are living with the darkness of disappointment, sadness, and loss? Do we seek His face for our energy and strength? Does God's face shine upon us as we go about the routines and busyness of life on earth? Is my face radiant because I look upward at the Son? Even on sunny days, I still have to choose to open my blinds or to go outdoors to reap the benefit of the sun. In the same way, I need to choose to let the Son into my life each day. Admittedly, sometimes I do not open the blinds of my house or of my soul. And when I make that choice, I am the one who misses the blessing.

When I think of heaven, which I now do far more frequently than I ever did before, I think of a place that is brilliantly aglow all of the time. One day I will see Jesus face to face, and it will be far more glorious than the brightest sun that adorns the morning sky. The Word tells us that His face will be like the sun shining in all its brilliance (Revelation 1:16). So how can I not think about the Son when I look at the sun? I love the early morning reminder from God that He is here, that I am not alone, and that He is going to follow me all day long, giving me grace and peace for the day (Numbers 6:24-26). The Son brings restoration (Psalm 80:3). He is gracious to the lonely and afflicted (Psalm 25:15, 16). Fixing my eyes on the Son gives me the power to overcome growing weary and losing heart (Hebrews 12:3). The Son is the radiance of God's glory, sustaining us by His powerful Word (Hebrews 1:3). He never takes His eyes off the righteous (Job 36:7).

Neither the sun that graces our world nor the Son who sits at the right hand of our Father in Heaven should be ignored. There is one difference between them: we should protect ourselves from the sun. In contrast, we can never get too many Son-rays. Do not turn away from the Son. Lord, make me radiant with Your grace and peace as You shine Your face on me.

> *Those who look to Him are radiant.*
> —Psalm 34:5a

> *The Lord bless you and keep you; the Lord make His face shine upon you and be gracious to you; the Lord turn His face toward you and give you peace.*
> —Numbers 6:24-26

Lord, make me radiant. Next time you look at the sun, ask yourself, "Does my face reflect the radiance of the Son?" Ask God to help you radiate Jesus.

44

Think About It

I think I can. I think I can. I think I can. The children's book *The Little Engine That Could*[9] tells the story of a little engine that uses a good dose of self-talk to climb a seemingly insurmountable mountain. Experiences like this, in which we accomplish a difficult task, reach a challenging goal, or overcome a fear that immobilized us in the past, gives us I-did-it moments that are well worth celebrating.

I had a great I-did-it morning this week. It's that time of year. We all have to face it: tax season. This inescapable obligation was one of the first daunting tasks that I had to address right after my husband's death. I was fearful and anxious because I had chosen to be ignorant and uninvolved in the process of filing taxes for the four decades of our married life. Although I am far from fully understanding tax rules and regulations, this time around I was very pleased to have adequately prepared all the necessary facts, figures, and forms for my meeting with the tax accountant. No pounding heart, no racing pulse, no tension headache like last year. I felt great satisfaction as I got into my car after the meeting, and thought to myself, *I did it!*

---

9   Watty Pipler, *The Little Engine That Could* (New York: Platt & Munk, 1930).

One of the biggest things that affects how I perceive a situation, whether it's a pleasant or a challenging one, is my own thoughts. What I tell myself about the situation impacts my approach and response to it. My husband was a good listener when I processed my thoughts out loud. He calmed me when my thoughts made me anxious. He helped me see other possibilities when my thoughts were skewed. He described a bigger picture when my perspective was myopic.

A person who lives alone talks to herself a lot. I have been thinking about the thoughts that fuel my self-talk. If I tell myself, *I don't think I can do that,* then I probably will not be able to do whatever that task might be. However, if I tell myself, *I think I can,* then there is a much higher possibility that I will successfully tackle the task or challenge that I face. If I tell myself, *I don't think I can survive without my husband,* then every day is going to be a challenge. If I tell myself, *I think I can do this with God's help*, then I will again find my place in His world. Recently, I made a list of the positive things my husband would want me to think, feel, or do. This was valuable exercise for me. It is helping me strengthen my I-think-I-can attitude.

The Bible has good advice for our thoughts and meditations. The psalmist, who seemed to suffer some sleep issues, tells us what he does when he lies awake at night. "On my bed I remember You; I think of You through the watches of the night" (Psalm 63:6). "My eyes stay open through the watches of the night, that I may meditate on Your promises" (Psalm 119:148). I admit that I have had a lot of waking hours when I wished I were sleeping; these were moments when my thought-life went into overdrive. However, it is not all bad. When it is just me and God, there are sweet moments as I meditate on who He is and what He is doing in my life. Even in loss, we have blessings; we will see them when we intentionally look for them, when we choose to think about His promises and His presence, when we deliberately focus on that which is excellent or praiseworthy.

Paul, in his book to the Philippians, follows up a sentence about anxiety with a list of positive things to think about in order to experience God's peace. There is nothing I would rather have than that kind of peace. Controlling the mind and channeling thoughts are foundational to receiving God's sweet peace. My breath prayer is that I think about praiseworthy things.

Finally brothers, whatever is true, whatever is noble, whatever is right, whatever is pure, whatever is lovely, whatever is admirable—if anything is excellent or praiseworthy—think about such things. And the God of peace will be with you.
—Philippians 4:8, 9b

May the words of my mouth and the meditation of my heart be pleasing in Your sight, O Lord, my Rock and my Redeemer.
—Psalm 19:14

Lord, help me think about good things. What or who comes to your mind when you think of each of the following: something that is true, something that is noble, something that is right, something that is pure, something that is lovely, something that is admirable, and something that is praiseworthy? What thoughts help you experience God's peace?

45

Shadow

Happy Groundhog's Day! I missed hearing those endearing words this week. You might wonder why Groundhog's Day would be such a big deal. Every February 2nd, my husband and I used to faithfully and playfully wish one another a happy Groundhog's Day. The reason? Groundhog's Day had a much deeper meaning for us than the possible appearance of a furry animal and a prediction of how much longer winter would last. On Groundhog's Day forty-three years ago, my husband-to-be placed a diamond ring on my finger and we announced to our family and friends that we were going to get married. Last year, we exchanged our Groundhog's Day salutations with mixed emotions, grateful for the many years we had shared together and somber because we knew it was the last year we would say it to one another.

There is no Punxsutawney Phil to predict how long the winter of grief will last. Just when those of us who are grieving think the season of feeling sad and alone and wanting to hibernate might be over, something happens to squelch that hope. Something frightens us, surprises us, or stirs up a memory, and then, like a groundhog scared of his shadow, we want to crawl back into our burrow and wrap ourselves in a blanket of memories as we let the unstoppable tears flow. We must remember on days like this that the current season might still be transitioning into the new season; perhaps we are just having a stormy day.

Perhaps, like me, you are affected by the climate and weather as you deal with situations and circumstances in your life. This week, a combination of ice, wind, snow, and frigid temperatures clouded my spirit. When I cannot escape the frostbite of grief, my home feels like the safest place to be, and my husband's prayer shawl protects me like warm clothing shields my body from the frigid outdoors.

My husband always did his best to protect me. If I was floating on an air mattress on the lake, he would make sure no one playfully pushed me into the water because he knew I would panic. One day, he came by with the truck to rescue me from my early morning walk because he had been awakened by thunder and had seen storm clouds ready to burst with rain. He shielded me whenever he could from circumstances and situations that would endanger me or hurt me. I felt safe in the shadow of his presence and his care. I miss the security of knowing his eyes and ears were on the alert for my well-being. I miss the refuge and protection he provided me in the sanctuary of his love and care. I miss the sparkle in his eye and the grin on his face when he looked at me and said things like "Happy Groundhog's Day."

I can no longer hide in the shadow of protection my husband provided. His death has forced me to be more intentional about dwelling in the shelter of the Most High. I know that God cares about me as much as—no, much more than—my husband did. I pray for rest in the shadow of His wings where I feel His unfailing love. The assurance of God's presence and protection soothes my mind, my heart, and my soul as I read His Word in the shelter of silence and solitude that my home provides on my personal Groundhog Days, days when my sadness makes me scared of my own shadow.

Keep me as the apple of Your eye; hide me in the shadow of Your wings.

—Psalm 17:8

Have mercy on me, O God, have mercy on me, for in You my soul takes refuge. I will take refuge in the shadow of Your wings until the disaster has passed.

—Psalm 57:1

He who dwells in the shelter of the Most High will rest in the shadow of the Almighty.

—Psalm 91:1

Lord, keep me in your shadow. What do you do when the shadow of disappointment, sorrow, worry, fear, anxiety, or angst assaults you? What comfort or peace have you experienced when you hid in the shadow of the Almighty?

46

Rise Up, Stand Firm

Learning to drive. Do you remember when you first got behind the driver's seat, turned the key in the ignition, put the vehicle in drive, and started to move forward? Although I grew up on a farm, I never drove the tractor or the pickup truck. We did not have a four-wheeler. I had a bicycle. That was the extent of my experience behind the wheel. Then I turned fifteen. Since my cousin had no more experience than I did, my aunt took us to the pasture for our first driving experience before we started Driver's Education. Our first orientation included starting, stopping, and driving in circles in the open pasture.

Fast-forward fifteen years: my husband bought a well-used car to serve as a second vehicle. Soon to be known as "the ugly green Fiat," it looked like a box on wheels. It had a manual transmission. No big deal; it was the car he drove. That is, until the day I had to take it home from church. It was parked at the side of the street, facing uphill, so I had to manage shifting gears as I did the clutch-gas-brake dance in such a way that I could get the car away from the curb and moving forward. Needless to say, the men who were standing outside the church enjoyed every minute of my humiliating experience. I am sure they enjoyed telling others about their pastor's wife's ineptness at driving a stick-shift vehicle. Difficult and embarrassing though it was, I was determined. I was motivated. I had to get home.

I knew no more about how to navigate through grief than I knew about driving a car the day my aunt took us to the pasture. Moving forward with grief is as jerky a ride as my first time driving our Fiat. It is quite a miserable ride, but it is a process that does eventually get one from point A to point B. Driving a car, even a stick shift, becomes easier with experience. Navigating life as a surviving spouse also begins to feel more comfortable with the passing of time and the accumulation of successful accomplishments. I am learning how to shift gears more smoothly as I traverse this road of grief.

One day, my husband came home with a cute little blue Honda in place of the ugly green Fiat. I was ecstatic! I got inside the car and my bubble of excitement burst immediately as my eyes beheld a lever between the front seats. I looked down. Sure enough, there was a gas pedal, a brake pedal *and* a clutch! *How could he?* I was not happy. But I took it for a drive. Unbelievable! I was able to flawlessly shift from one gear to the next; the ride was not at all jerky. The combination of my learning to drive the Fiat and now having a better car made a world of difference in my manual-transmission driving competency.

It has been almost a year since I first found myself behind the wheel of widowhood, driving in circles around the barren field of life, afraid and overwhelmed. Nothing was automatic. Everything required a clutch-gas-brake dance. Without a choice in the matter, I started Griever's Education, doing the book-work in the privacy of my home and on-the-road driving practice in public, venturing out onto both old and new roads. Things are starting to change. The ride is smoothing out. It does not feel like the road is always uphill, or that I am just jolting back and forth. Some things have now become automatic for me. Others still need to be manually shifted, but I am learning the process and becoming more confident. Persistently praying the names of the Lord has carried me through the ruggedness of grief. It is empowering me to rise up and stand firm as I trust the Lord to carry me through the day.

> *Some trust in chariots and some in horses* (or ugly green Fiats) *but we trust in the name of the Lord our God. They are brought to their knees and fall, but we rise up and stand firm.*
>
> —Psalm 20:7-8

Lord, help me rise up and stand firm. What names of the Lord cause you to rise up and stand firm?

47

Strength

I do not want a north-facing driveway. I can still hear my husband saying this to our realtor as we began our house search. Homeowners know that, when buying a house, one cannot always get everything on their want and do-not-want list. I got a north-facing driveway along with my new house. Memories of these wise words came back like a clanging cymbal this week when I spent hours trying to get ice off the driveway. Thankfully, two of my young grandchildren diligently worked with me. Thankfully, a kind neighbor brought me a product that was quite effective for melting ice. Thankfully, the temperature was mild so I could enjoy being outdoors. I had to search for everything that I was thankful for because I wanted to give up, go inside, and have a good cry. The cry came later, I will admit. I missed my husband. He would have done this for me. I missed my old house. The driveway did not face north.

My body aches. My heart aches. My husband had strong hands and incredible endurance. I am not as strong as he was, physically or emotionally. Memories of my husband's declining health, of my first Valentine's Day without my beloved, and the ice-covered driveway sent me into an emotional downward spiral this week.

My breath prayer became a plea for strength. Physical experts promote the value of strength training based on the premise that what is used develops, whereas that which is not used wastes away. We can read about the advantages of strength training, look at advertisements for it, and watch commercials that entice us to join fitness centers. However, no matter how much we learn about strength training and no matter how good our intentions are, unless we *do* something about it, the knowledge does us no good. And if we choose to begin a strength-training regimen, we will not reap long-term benefits unless we stick with the program.

What is true of physical strength training is also true of spiritual strength training: only that which is used develops. The best thing I did for my spiritual training this past year was to obey these words of Scripture: "Be still and wait on the Lord" (Psalms 46:10; 27:14). This week I feel emotionally weak. My heart aches. The pain that comes from the loss of a spouse is deep because in a marital relationship, two people become one flesh. You strengthen one another when you are together. Grief intensifies one's faith-workout. *That which is used develops.* I am developing stronger faith and deeper trust in the sovereignty of the Almighty God.

I no longer have that special person with whom I started and ended the day, shared several cups of coffee, talked about and prayed for our future, our family, our church, and our world. This is a huge void. I have had to work my way through so many things needing to be done and decisions needing to be made, all of them new endeavors for me. First-time experiences take a lot of energy. How did I get up each morning and do what needed to be done? I know that the Lord gave me the strength to walk and not faint. No, I never ran, and yes, I did get weary (Isaiah 41:30-31). I did not volunteer for this intense faith-training regimen. I am grateful that I have a Master Strength Trainer who never leaves my side, tells me what He expects of me, gently guides me along the course and, unlike any physical strength trainer, carries me when I cannot take another step.

The Bible would not tell us to train ourselves to be godly (1 Timothy 4:7) if it came naturally. I will be in training all my life. I pray for strength.

> *Look to the Lord and His strength; seek His face always.*
> —Psalm 105:4

> *But He said to me, "My grace is sufficient for you, for My power is made perfect in weakness."*
> —2 Corinthians 12:9a

> *For the eyes of the Lord range throughout the earth to strengthen those whose hearts are fully committed to Him.*
> —2 Chronicles 16:9a

Lord, give me strength. What does your spiritual strength training regimen involve? Do you have an icy north-facing driveway that challenges your stamina? How is God making your faith muscles stronger?

48

Surrender

It's my turn! Children learn to take turns at a young age. They like the idea when it is their turn! But sometimes it is not your turn. Adults also need to accept the fact that sometimes it is not our turn. We like it when it is our turn and we get what we want. But no one wants to take their turn when the *getting* is something we do not want, like the death of someone we love, the loss of a business, or a broken relationship.

Taking turns is an act of surrender. Healthy relationships develop when people are willing to surrender the right to be right all of the time. Sometimes it is not our turn; we need to surrender the right to always have things done the way we think they should be done.

Painful and unwelcome though my loss has been, it has led me to do the hard work of more fully surrendering to God's divine plan and accepting His control over my life. Surrendering has not been a one-time act. It is something I have had to do repeatedly. Why? Because I have a habit of taking back the very things I have previously surrendered to God. Then I struggle again with right and wrong, fair and unfair, until I am miserable. Peace returns only when I surrender. Relinquishing my right to have things the way I would choose them to be has brought a deeper relationship with Jesus Christ.

My husband and I dreamed about what we would do when we retired. We had hopes and plans. They always included *us*, never just me or just him. The words of "Jesus, all for Jesus"[10] was, and continues to be, an expression of my personal commitment to serve God wholeheartedly: "All of my ambitions, hopes, and plans, I surrender these into Your hands." I find comfort in the next phrase: "For it's only in Your will that I am free." Although my dreams are shattered, I believe that I will continue to see God's plan for my life unfold as I surrender to Him and respond to the opportunities He bestows. I will keep on singing: "Jesus, all for Jesus, all I am and have and ever hope to be."

When we stick with personal resolutions and goals, surrendering old practices and developing new habits, we reap long-term benefits. Surrendering to the Lord in life and in death, when life is fair and when it is unfair, when it is our turn and when it is not, leads us to experience the peace and freedom that we receive when we trust His sovereign plan for our lives.

Surrender. Submit. It is not your turn. It is your turn. The context determines whether taking our turn is exciting or difficult.

A year ago, we were facing the reality that it would soon be my husband's turn to go to heaven. As I think about the final weeks of his life on earth, about my first year of life without him by my side, and about the years ahead for me, I know I must surrender. Love is all about surrender. Surrender is the key to a loving relationship, to our love for others, to our love for God, and to God's love for us. After all, that's what Jesus did on the cross: He surrendered.

---

[10]   Robin Mark, "Jesus, All for Jesus" (Word Music, 1990).

Sometimes it is our turn, and sometimes it is not. Surrender reaps reward. God asks me to surrender to His will. He promises that He will lift me up and lead me through life until the day comes when it is my turn to go to the mansion He has prepared for me.

> *Submit yourselves, then, to God. Humble yourselves before the Lord, and He will lift you up. You ought to say, "If it is the Lord's will, we will live and do this or that."*
> —James 4:7a, 10, 15

> *Teach me to do Your will, for You are my God; may Your good Spirit lead me on level ground.*
> —Psalm 143:10

Lord, help me surrender. In what situations in your life do you need to surrender? Is there a relationship in which you need to give up or take your turn? Have you fully surrendered every detail of your life to God?

49

Transform

Really, another trip to Menards? I like to shop, but something is skewed when I look at my credit card bill and see more charges from home improvement stores than clothing or department stores! Recent shopping sprees have brought me down aisles to look for items that, a year ago, I had no idea even existed! I am undergoing a major homeowner transformation. No longer can I be an indifferent bystander, trusting that my husband will eventually do what needs to be done. I'm learning a lot as I transition into the life of a single woman who is determined to take care of herself.

There are a variety of tools on the workbench in my garage. Although they all have names, my ability to identify tools is limited to hammer, screwdriver, pliers, and level. I have examined odd-looking items on the workbench a number of times, trying to find one that might help me accomplish what I want to do. It does not really matter to me whether I'm using the tool actually designed for the given task as long as it gets the job done. I am proud to say I did personally buy my first tool; I now own a stud finder! I did not even know such a tool existed until I saw someone else using one. Then I decided it would be a good thing for me to have. After all, I want to be able to hang wall décor myself, and I doubt that I will ever be able to find studs by just tapping on the wall.

Shopping at home improvement stores and going to appointments with attorneys, bankers, insurance agents, and car servicemen are some of the changes that have transpired in my life this past year. In reality, these were the easy ones. Much harder were changes like attending worship services alone, going to social gatherings by myself, and carving out a new kind of life as a single woman.

It has been a year of transformation. Life turned upside down and inside out and I am changed. My circumstances are different from what they used to be. My perspective has changed. My desires have been fine-tuned. My seeking of God has intensified. My heart and soul have a greater desire than ever before to be transformed into the likeness of my Lord. I have pleaded with God to show me His will. I had, in years past, experienced life detours because of unexpected situations, but the death of my husband is by far the most devastating and life-changing situation in my life. Trials lead me to question God's purpose and plan. What I have discovered is that God seldom reveals the exact details of my comings and goings. However, my response is very important to Him. God's will is that I respond to whatever happens in my life with the characteristics and attitudes of a Spirit-filled person.

Extreme makeovers have become popular in our society. The subjects of makeovers are diverse: houses, businesses, bodies, clothing. Even churches undergo extreme makeovers. This happened in my community years ago when Dutch-speaking services transitioned to English-speaking services. We now live in an era when traditional services are being transformed into contemporary, modern, or nontraditional services.

Crises cause people to undergo extreme makeovers. Accidents strip people and possessions from us. Death claims lives and leaves families changed. We may be devastated by what happened to us, but we do not need to be destroyed. My breath prayer is that in this time of weeping and mourning, God transforms my mind, heart, and will to be like

His. I pray that through my extreme makeover I will become a more fully devoted follower of Jesus, faithfully loving God above all and my neighbor as myself.

> *There is a time for everything. to be born and a time to die, a time to weep and a time to laugh, a time to mourn and a time to dance.*
>
> —Ecclesiastes 3:1a, 2a, 4

> *Do not conform any longer to the pattern of this world, but be transformed by the renewing of your mind. Then you will be able to test and approve what God's will is—His good, pleasing and perfect will.*
>
> —Romans 12:2

> *And we, who with unveiled faces all reflect the Lord's glory, are being transformed into His likeness with ever-increasing glory, which comes from the Lord, who is the Spirit.*
>
> —2 Corinthians 3:18

Lord, transform me. What is causing your extreme makeover? How are you choosing to respond? What changes are you seeing as you are being transformed into the likeness of Christ? What transformational work still needs to happen in the renewal of your mind?

50

I Am With You

There, that's done. I have said this many times—sometimes aloud, sometimes just in my head—after a big event, a special worship service, or a challenging situation. This declaration holds feelings of accomplishment as well as relief after hours of preparation and anticipation.

Many times this year, after having signed a paper, made a phone call, or gone to an appointment, I have said to myself, *I hope that's finished now.* I am a starter and a finisher. I do not like unfinished projects. I meet deadlines. Yet there are things in life that do not have a finish date or finish line, but are open-ended—like grief.

Grief has no finish line. At the end of one year, the thing in your life called "grief" cannot be packed up and stored away. There is no protocol for grief, no list of things to do in order to finish grieving. There are no rules to guide a griever from one level to the next until he has scored the winning point. Incompleteness is one of the dynamics that makes grief messy. There is no timetable for grief. There is no formula for grief that guarantees success. Grief has no blueprint.

So what do we do with this ugly thing called grief? It is acc/ wear it for a while, but then people tire of seeing it on you. We, too, g- tired of the sadness, the sorrow, the loneliness. We get better at hiding it when we are around others, but when we take off our masks, it is still there. We try to ignore it. Like a drippy faucet, it becomes an annoying nemesis when we are alone. We get angry, we feel sad, we become frustrated, and finally we withdraw because we do not know what to do with this new permanent aspect of our lives.

We can expect to have troubles as long as we live on earth. Jesus said, "In this world you will have trouble" (John 16:33). Although we might not have the ability to resolve, remove, or replace our loss, or to turn our circumstances right side up again, we do have the option to make wise choices about how we respond to our situation. Life might center around our loss for a season. At some point, we must resume living. I did not want to look back and realize that I had not adequately grieved. But I did not know how to grieve; I went to support groups, read books, and talked with others who had also suffered loss. Although praying audibly was difficult for me, my conversation with God flowed easily when I wrote down my words of lament and sorrow, when I penned my desire for comfort and peace. Through breath-prayer words and the supporting verses of Scripture, I discovered strength and restoration. Over and over, I heard God say, "I am with you."

On the cross, Jesus said, "It is finished" (John 19:30). Those three words are music to my ears. They are words of hope. He finished His work as our Savior, and because of that, I know that my loss, though I will grieve it for the remainder of my days on earth, is temporary. Heaven awaits me because Jesus said, "There that's done!"

Fear not, for I have redeemed you; I have called you by name; you are Mine. When you pass through the waters, I will be with you; and when you pass through the rivers, they will not sweep over you. When you walk through the fire, you will not be burned; the flames will not set you ablaze. For I am the Lord, your God. Do not be afraid, for I am with you.

—Isaiah 43:2-3a, 5a

Lord, help me to remember You are with me. Many people deal with situations that are too painful, shameful, or private to share. What brings you grief? What brings you comfort? What is good medicine for your soul to reduce the ache of your loss and rehabilitate your broken spirit? Do you hear God say, "I am with you"?

51

To God Be the Glory

Home forever. One year ago, my husband went to dwell in the glory of heaven, his eternal home where he now resides with the King of Kings and Lord of Lords. The garments of imperfection and suffering in which he was clothed on earth have been replaced with a robe of righteousness and a crown of life (Isaiah 61:10; James 1:12). He has been crowned with glory and honor (Hebrews 2:7).

I cannot even begin to fathom what this year has been like for him. I picture him worshiping His Savior and Lord and talking with the patriarchs, prophets, and disciples. I can just hear him saying to them, "I loved preaching about you!" I imagine him, adventurous as he was, exploring heaven and stopping to meet and greet family and friends as well as people from the ends of the earth.

Reflecting on Jim's life and death reminds me of what often happened when we took long bike rides. It was common for him to reach our destination ahead of me. There he would patiently wait for me to catch up, cheering for me as I arrived at the finish line. One year ago, he reached the finish line in the race of life. It is taking me longer to finish the race, but the day is coming when I will cross the finish line into Heaven and he will be there, cheering for me as I, too, arrive at our eternal destination.

Although I would not have chosen this path for my life, God has blessed me with His power and His presence. He is healing my broken heart. Through His Spirit at work in me, I have received courage, strength, protection, and hope as I grieve the loss of my dearly beloved and move forward into living life on earth without him.

Memories live in our hearts forever. They are all you have left after someone dies. Since memories fade over time, it is good to preserve them with pictures, stories, and written words. Today I reflect on Jim's interests, passions, and relationships as I observe the one-year anniversary of Jim's meeting Jesus face to face. I have written about these memories as a tribute to my beloved husband, James LeRoy Hoogeveen, whose life on earth reflected the heart of a man who passionately loved God and cared deeply about people. I share these very personal reflections, my "Jimisms," with you. Some of you who read this knew my husband; you will smile or nod your head as you read. Those who never got to meet him will get a glimpse into the life of a man who finished well. My breath prayer is that in life and death, I, too, will be willing and able to say, "To God be the glory!"

> *For from Him and through Him and to Him are all things. To Him be the glory forever! Amen.*
> —Romans 11:36

> *"Hallelujah! Salvation and glory and power belong to our God."*
> —Revelation 19:1b

> *Ascribe to the Lord the glory due His name; worship the Lord in the splendor of His holiness.*
> — Psalm 29:2

God, to You be the glory! What are your reflections on people you love, people who have impacted your life? Is it time for you to pen your memories and perhaps to share them before death strikes? What do you want people to see in the reflection of your heart? What are you intentionally doing in order to give God the glory in your life?

My Reflections

James LeRoy Hoogeveen
(March 4, 1950-March 2, 2012)

1. He loved God above all and his neighbor as himself.
2. He loved me deeply and expressed his love by taking care of me, providing for me, and watching out for my good. He encouraged me to use my spiritual gifts, natural talents, and developed skills. He challenged me to be a godly woman.
3. He loved his children and grandchildren and was involved in their lives. He had the privilege of officiating at the wedding ceremonies of all three of his children and of baptizing all seven of his grandchildren.
4. He was an evangelist. He wanted people to know Jesus; he felt called to be God's servant, to preach the gospel of Jesus Christ, to train leaders, and to serve others in myriad ways.
5. He was an ordained minister for thirty-five years. He was the pastor of three established churches, served as the founding pastor of two new churches, and developed and directed a Leadership Development Network for lay leaders.
6. He had passion for building God's kingdom. He assisted the process of planting a church behind the walls and creating a ministry for immigrants. He mentored numerous seminarians, pastors, and leaders who were serving God according to their specific gifts and callings.

7. He was innovative, self-motivated, and industrious. He lived life with gusto. He worked hard, played hard, and exercised hard.

8. He had an on/off switch. Seldom did he toss and turn at night because of the challenges experienced by him personally or by those he was helping. He entrusted them to the Lord, knowing the importance of sleep to refresh his body and renew his mind.

9. He believed that few good decisions are made after 10:00 p.m. Therefore, he was known for leading meetings that did not linger into the late hours of the night.

10. He was adventurous, which was evident in his work, hobbies, and travels.

11. He was an avid reader. His reading repertoire was extensive and diverse.

12. He knew how to relax. He had a special coffee mug that he used on Saturdays, his day off. It says, "Nothing would be finer than sitting in my recliner."

13. A relaxing evening for him consisted of sitting in his recliner, watching sports, reading a book or magazine, and eating *Planters* cocktail peanuts.

14. He replaced his IBM Selectric electric typewriter with his first computer in 1982. He stayed current with advances in technology and helped many people to set up and to learn how to use their home computers.

15. He was a handyman, troubleshooter, and do-it-yourself guy. The only home improvement professionals he readily hired were painters. He did not like to paint!

16. He was wise and skilled in many different facets of life. He invited opportunities to share his experience and knowledge with our children, family, and friends.

17. He contributed to the well-being of the communities in which he lived. He served as an emergency medical technician, a faith-step counselor for Alcoholics Anonymous, a hospital chaplain, and a chamber of commerce diplomat.

18. He chose to be content in sickness and in health, in richness and in poverty, in flourishing ministries and in struggling ones, when life was going smoothly and when there were challenges. He chose to rejoice in God for whatever He gave and to block the influx of negativity that so easily fills the human heart and mind.

19. He kept a record of the messages that he preached from January, 1976 through December, 2011. The first message was entitled "Salt for Flavor, Light for Seeing" (Matthew 5:13-16). Thirty-five years later, his last message—after he knew he had cancer and less than three months before his death—was "To God Be the Glory" (Ephesians 3:14-21).

For this reason, I kneel before the Father, from whom His whole family in heaven and on earth derives its name. I pray that out of His glorious riches He may strengthen you with power through His Spirit in your inner being, so that Christ may dwell in your hearts through faith. And I pray that you, being rooted and established in love, may have power, together with all the saints, to grasp how wide and long and high and deep is the love of Christ, and to know this love that surpasses knowledge—that you may be filled to the measure of all the fullness of God. Now to Him who is able to do immeasurable more than all we ask or imagine, according to His power that is at work with us, to Him be glory in the church and in Christ Jesus throughout all generations, forever and ever! Amen.

—Ephesians 3:14-21

52

Peace

Surprise! Some people love surprises. Others do not like being caught off guard. Life is full of surprises, both good and bad, happy and disappointing. You might be certain beyond the shadow of a doubt that something is going to be great, but it could still turn out to be a complete disaster. You might get up in the morning, knowing you are doomed to have a horrible day, but by nightfall lay your head on the pillow, still amazed at the positive turn in the day's events. Life is, indeed, full of surprises.

I had anticipated that this week, the one-year anniversary of my husband's final days on earth and first moments in heaven, would inevitably be a time of intense grieving. I expected feelings of despair and devastation. God surprised me. Day after day this dreaded week, I felt an incredible spirit of serenity and quietude. Tears did not cloud my eyes, nor did sorrow hinder me from getting out of bed. My soul was wrapped in a tranquil blanket of peace.

I went to the cemetery and stood by Jim's grave, reflecting on our life together. I visited with all of my children and many family members and friends. Reading the posts and the guestbook on my husband's CaringBridge website, I reflected on our journey through cancer and death. I was comforted and encouraged by the overwhelming support our family received from the Body of Christ. People encouraged me with emails and beautiful sympathy cards. I read all the Scriptures and verses written in the hundreds of cards. I watched the video recording of my husband's Celebration of Life service. I sat at my piano and played the songs we had sung at the service, letting the lyrics remind me that in life and in death, I have hope in Christ alone. We ate some of my husband's favorite foods and reminisced about happy times and precious memories.

God, who is able to do immeasurably more than all we ask or imagine (Ephesians 3:20), blessed me with a spirit of peace on the one-year anniversary of my husband's Homecoming. I know Jim is in heaven with the Lord. I also know the Lord is with me here on earth, living in my life through the power of His Holy Spirit. My mourning will continue. I will not be surprised to experience days of sadness in the future. However, at this moment, I am thankful for a peace that is beyond my understanding. Over and over this past year, I have prayed for peace. Although I believe that God answers prayer, I must admit I was amazed this week to receive the answer to this prayer at this time. I was surprised by peace. That's a wonderful surprise!

I love the beautiful benediction my husband was privileged to proclaim for thirty-five years:

> *"The Lord bless you and keep you;*
> *The Lord make His face shine upon you*
> *and be gracious to you;*
> *The Lord turn His face toward you*
> *And give you peace."*
>
> —Numbers 6:24-26

The Lord has blessed me. The Lord has been gracious to me. The Lord has given me peace. Praise the Lord!

*You will keep in perfect peace him whose mind is steadfast,
because he trusts in You.*

—Isaiah 26:3

*And the peace of God, which transcends all understanding,
will guard your hearts and your minds in Christ Jesus.*

—Philippians 4:7

*Peace I leave with you; My peace I give you. I do not give
to you as the world gives. Do not let your hearts be troubled
and do not be afraid.*

—John 14:27

*Now may the Lord of peace Himself give you peace at all
times and in every way. The Lord be with all of you.*

—2 Thessalonians 3:16

Lord, give me peace. Do you long for peace? Praise God for a time when
you experienced His peace in a manner that transcended explanation
or measurement.

Keep Going. Do Not Stop. Breathe.

Keep going. Do not stop. Put one foot in front of the other. Breathe. These were the words of a young man who encouraged many of us, all of us old enough to be his parents, as we climbed steep hills and ascended hundreds of steps on our Holy Land tour. This twenty-year-old football player's advice, passed down from his coach, has been my mantra often since that trip, especially as I walked through the valley of the shadow of death.

I had to intentionally put one foot in front of the other this past year. I had to keep going. I had to breathe. We had come alongside many who grieved in our years of ministry. However, when I was the one grieving, I experienced dynamics of sorrow that I had not previously understood. Although the details of loss differ from person to person, a griever's emotions and experiences may follow similar patterns. I have shared what I am learning as I live with grief and I pray that it provides encouragement and comfort to someone else who needs healing from loss. Maybe my description of grief will heighten your understanding of and sensitivity to someone who is walking in the valley of loss. A person's response to grief is neither right nor wrong. It is his or her own reality. Grief, like fingerprints, is unique to every individual.

It was in the silence and solitude of the valley of death that I learned my greatest lessons about myself, about my relationships with people, and about my Almighty God. Breath praying through this painful year has enriched my relationship with the Lord Jesus Christ. Single words repeated throughout the day kept me focused on the presence of the Lord and the power of His Word and Spirit in me.

At creation, God breathed into man and he became a living being. From the very beginning, God displayed His desire for a personal relationship with mankind by creating us in His image and by breathing His life into us. Shortly before Jesus ascended back to Heaven, He breathed on the disciples and told them to receive the Holy Spirit. Breath is the essence of life—both physical and spiritual life.

What did I do when my world turned upside down and inside out? How did I respond when I lost someone very precious to me? I breathed single words to the One who hears every word. I breathed in God's presence. I breathed out my fears and anxieties. I said many breath prayers. They have given me comfort, strength, and hope as I mourned my loss. My spiritual journey continues. And so must I. I must remember my young friend's words: "Keep going. Do not stop. Breathe." Above all, I must remember my Heavenly Father's words: "Be still, and know that I am God!"

> *And the Lord God formed man from the dust of the ground and breathed into his nostrils the breath of life, and man became a living being.*
> —Genesis 2:7

> *And Jesus said, "Peace be with you! As the Father has sent Me, I am sending you." And with that He breathed on them and said, "Receive the Holy Spirit."*
> —John 20:21-22

> *Then you will call, and the Lord will answer; you will cry for help, and He will say: Here am I.*
> —Isaiah 58:9

Be still, and know that I am God.

—Psalm 46:10a

Lord, help me breathe Your words. What impact has breath praying had on you? Keep going. Do not stop. Breathe. What new breath prayer words is the Holy Spirit giving to you?

Walking Through the Valley of the Shadow of Death

My Beliefs, Feelings, and Discoveries

My grief and pain are mine. Only in feeling them do
I open myself to the lessons they can teach.
—Anne Wilson Schaef

Faith, Hope, and Love

1. Death is sacred for those who believe Jesus Christ is their Lord and Savior.
2. The ache of sorrow is very deep but the presence of God is very real.
3. My Heavenly Father knew, on the day I said my wedding vows, that I would be the surviving spouse.
4. Surrendering and submitting to God's divine plan brings comfort, strength, and freedom.
5. Joy and sorrow can coexist when you trust the sovereignty of God.
6. Pain and suffering are temporary. Hope, founded in Christ, is eternal.

Even when I feel abandoned and alone, I know I am not. God keeps His promise to never leave me or forsake me. He is always present through His Holy Spirit and often through caring people. E-mails, cards, and phone calls are life-giving nourishment for a grieving soul.

8. The Body of Christ is much broader than my geographic circle of people.

9. People do not need to use words to tell me they care. Presence is powerful.

10. Treasure people, not things. Do not let the tensions and anxieties of living with imperfect people in this imperfect world diminish your ability to enjoy the people who love you and whom you love. You never know when their life on this earth, or yours, will be over.

11. As much as possible, live without regrets so you can die without regrets.

> *The Lord gave and the Lord has taken away; may the name of the Lord be praised.*
> —Job 1:21b

Word and Prayer

12. Praying a single word, a *breath prayer*, has become my lifeline to the One who gives me life. Although I cannot possibly pray for everything that overwhelms my soul, I can breathe a single word over and over throughout the day as I face the different facets and realities of loss.

13. Bible verses bring comfort and power as they remind me of the very essence and presence of God, my Father.

14. Prayer is powerful. I have received good returns on everyone's prayer investments. God continues to answer prayers my husband prayed for me while he was still on earth.

My advocate is on high. My intercessor is my friend as my eyes pour out tears to God. I have treasured the words of His mouth more than my daily bread.

—Job 16:19b-20; 23:12b

Grief

15. Both dying and grieving are hard work. When the person who dies is a believer, he gets the best end of the deal. Death ends in victory. The sting of grief never goes away.

16. The nature of one's grieving is shaped by the relationship the person had with the one lost, the personality traits of the person grieving, and the dynamics surrounding the loss.

17. Crying comes in spurts. Sadness lasts all day long.

18. Grief is as unique as fingerprints, as snowflakes, as the people God created. There is no formula, no timetable, no protocol for grief. There is no one-size-fits-all program to get through grief.

19. Grieving can skew how one looks at things. A grieving person might be prone to dwelling on the past and resisting the future.

20. Grief is exhausting. It drains one physically, emotionally, and mentally. However, it also has the power to strengthen one's relationship with the Heavenly Father as we hold tightly to His loving presence, the security of His powerful sufficiency, and the hope of His saving grace.

21. Grief is messy. It takes patience for those who are grieving and for the family, friends, and coworkers of the one grieving.

22. Grievers may have attacks of jealousy. A griever might be jealous of the loved one who got to go to heaven first. A grieving parent may be jealous of parents who are busy with healthy children; a surviving spouse may be jealous of other couples who are enjoying life together. The best antidote for jealousy is naming

the many blessings you had in your relationship with your loved one, as well as the positive things that are still happening in your life.

23. The intensity of grieving may lighten, but I doubt that I will ever be finished grieving. I believe grieving is a lifelong reality when one suffers an extreme loss.

24. "How are you?" is a difficult question to answer. A grieving person does not have words to describe how he or she is. How I am can, in fact, change from one hour to the next.

25. Many who grieve long to hear others speak about their loved one. Hearing others share stories or memories reassures those mourning that their loved one has not been forgotten, that his life left an impact on others, and that others also miss him.

26. Anticipation of a first is sometimes worse than the event itself. Making specific plans for these difficult days is helpful.

My spirit is broken. My eyes have gown dim with grief.

—Job 17:1a, 7a

Life Changes

27. The loss of a spouse changes a person. *We* becomes *I*. *Our* becomes *my*. *Us* becomes *me*. Loss changes one's perspective, priorities, and purpose. I am being remodeled, reshaped, redefined. What does not change is the fact that I am a child of God, His treasured possession.

28. We may talk hypothetically about death with our spouses, saying things like "If I die—", "If you die—". However, if you are actually the survivor, the reality of how to finish those sentences may not be the same as you'd thought when you had those conversations. It is okay to make decisions that are different than ones my husband would have made. *My* situation is different than *our* situation was, and I have to act accordingly.

29. Asking myself what positive things would my husband want me to think, feel, and do has helped me make choices for my new kind of life.
30. Accepting the reality of my loved one's death is necessary for rediscovering true joy in the Lord. Embracing God's sovereignty in my life is foundational for experiencing His peace.

> *Yet if you devote your heart to Him and stretch out your hands to Him . . . you will stand firm and without fear . . . and darkness will become like morning.*
> —Job 11:13, 15b, 17

My Personal Breath Prayer Words

Develop your own personal breath prayer word list to help you more fully experience the presence of the Lord.

CPSIA information can be obtained at www.ICGtesting.com
Printed in the USA
LVOW08s0237151013

356880LV00003B/6/P